*"Shane's new book poses THE vital question of 2017, is accounting
software becoming too clever for our core business to survive?
If it is, what do we do about it? what about fee pressure?
What about staff competencies? What about winning new business.
In his typically practical and no-nonsense approach,
Shane looks at all these issues and more before proposing
implementable solutions to future proof your firm."*

– MARTIN BISSETT, Author of 'Passport to Partnership',
'Business Development On A Budget' and 'Winning Your First Client'.

*"There has never ever been a better time to be an accountant.
Accountants are the new rockstars of business – really. Cloud-based
accounting gives accountants unparalleled proactive firepower to assist
their clients real-time with timely, relevant and meaningful reporting.
Now you can do things like generate management accounts that enable
your clients to make prompt, informed, savvy business decisions.
Here's the issue though. Your clients believe that cloud-based accounting
puts them in the driver seat and somehow the accountant is redundant.
This is simply not true. The accountant is still the relationship interface
between data and success. No accounting programme can match the
qualifications, business experience and genuine bespoke interpretation
of data as it applies to a clients' business. As a business coach with a
global business I rely heavily on proactive accounting support to help my
clients make quantum leaps and get a dramatic uplift in their business.
If an accountant isn't across this material I move on and advise my
clients to switch accountant. Accountants have entered a highly
relational and niched era of client care. If you miss this key point you will
miss a massive win-fall. Shane Lukas has written the perfect accountant's
book for our times. This is up-to-the minute, on trend and on-message.
Read the book. Join his network and watch your practice sky-rocket".*

– ANDREW PRIESTLEY, Award winning Business Leadership Coach
and founder of The Coaching Experience (TCE).

*"Thanks technology – accounting will never be the same.
But, you don't need to get railroaded by the immensely changing space.
This book paves the way for accountants to leverage all that is
happening to take your practice to the highest levels ever".*

– MIKE MICHALOWICZ, author of 'Profit First'
and co-founder of Profit First Professionals.

*"This is a great book which every accountant who wants to stay in
business should read immediately. Shane has managed to condense
what can be a complicated subject into something any accountant
can understand but best of all it is all ACTIONABLE!"*

– SIMON CHAPLIN, Founder of Socks Up Simon, Award winning
practicing accountant and Adviser to the profession, UK.

*"This is possibly one of the best books for accountants to read.
It really explains both the biggest challenge facing them and at the
same times explains very clearly what and how they can change their
relationship with their client so that they become really valued. I have
always thought that understanding how people value what they want as
compared to what they need to be critical in any business relationship.
Accountants need to understand that in the future, their future is
dependent upon them providing what their clients want!"*

– JONATHAN HOLROYD, Author of 'Accountancy, it's your business',
Former partner at Hunter Gee Holroyd Accountants
and Adviser to the profession, UK.

*"Accounting practices are in such a powerful position to effect major
change across a wide section of the business community. Accountants
are a rare bread, being privy to the finances of the majority of global
business. Accountants can change the world. This book is awesome.
It leads the reader through the process of leveraging cloud accounting
as a tool to deliver new and exciting services based on leveraging the
core skills of accountants. I love how this book talks about the why and
them more importantly steps the reader through the how.
A must read for any partner in an accounting practice".*

– WAYNE SCHMIDT, Practice Adviser KarbonHQ, Australia.

What's Next For Accountants

*How to make the biggest threat
facing the profession
your biggest opportunity*

Shane Lukas

Copyright ©2017 Added Value Solutions, Shane Lukas

First published 2017 by Added Value Solutions,
7 Midland Way, Derbyshire, S43 4XA

This edition published 2017

A catalogue for this book is available in the British Library

Edited by Harriet Powney

Designed by Charles Bradshaw

Printed and bound in the UK

Paperback ISBN: 978-0-9551007-9-6
Kindle ISBN: 978-0-9551007-8-9

Contents

Contents

Appendix 1

Appendix 2

Appendix 3

Appendix 4

Appendix 5

Introduction

In this book I'll share with you everything you need to know in order to position yourself as the expert in the eyes of your customers and change their perception that you're 'just an accountant.'

I'll show you how to develop and deliver a business growth programme that's centred around your skills with numbers, helping you to help businesses you work with and improve them.

I'll teach you how to repurpose your skills as an accountant to become a truly valued business advisor.

And I'll share with you some key ideas that will improve any business.

Throughout, I'll be referencing additional learning and resources that you can access via the website **www.improveyourpractice.co.uk**. If you're an AVN member then you'll already have full access to all these and much more including training, high impact reporting tools and many shortcuts that will help apply many of the principles described in this book. If you'd like to learn more about AVN you're welcome to email me at **shane.lukas@avn.co.uk** or message me via LinkedIn.

Throughout this book I've provided some optional read personal examples which I've included with a grey highlighted text.

Please do connect with me on LinkedIn:
www.Linkedin.com/in/SLUKAS

I'd love to get your thoughts on this book and to hear about your progress. Or, if you have any questions, please don't hesitate to contact me.

Part 1
Step Up, Step Out Or Sign On

The impending death of the profession

Your world as an accountant is about to come crashing down. Compliance accounting produced by accountants is ending. Just as Google has replaced the role of many librarians, accountants who rely on income from producing compliance and management accounts face a bitter future as technology replaces them too...

UNLESS...

Read this book to discover why the profession is under threat, and what you can do to prevent it happening to you.

Why the profession will become obsolete

You'll be aware just how fast technology, and specifically accounting technology, has been advancing over the years. So far, this advancement has been favourable to those accountants who've embraced it. It's meant quicker turnaround times and easier migration from manual to computerised bookkeeping. Plus, the various bolt-ons available have meant easy integration with online payment tools, reduced error-checking time and management reports produced with a click. Effective reporting and even debt collection is made easy.

However, as much as this may have been of help to you so far, it now threatens your profession.

Imagine how many software companies around the world are currently racing to develop bolt-on software for the major accounts solution providers. In that race, every time a company

---

makes a breakthrough and develops a great feature, the others replicate it and build it in – adding it to the feature they were working on themselves. And so it continues, each company leap-frogging briefly ahead as more and more features are added to the software, most with the ultimate aim of replacing the role of the accountant completely. Removing the middleman or woman. Cutting out you.

Throughout history, how many trades have seen their demise because of technological advancements? Why should yours be any different?

I'm a big fan of technology. This book isn't designed to be anti-technology. It's about teaching you how to embrace and evolve with it.

Because, let's face it, it's not just accounting-based technology that threatens your profession. The rate the world is evolving is incredible. And to survive, we have to keep adapting to the ever-changing environment in which we live and do business.

The days are long gone when you could simply look back over your previous year's accounts in order to make sensible decisions going forward.

The word 'agile' is coming up more and more: agile strategy, agile project management, agile teams. Agile means the ability to move quickly and easily. In other words, creating a strategic plan and sticking to it rigidly has become pointless.

Looking at last year's accounts to make decisions about the current or coming year serves no real purpose to any business owner. Yet accountants are still delivering this service – no longer to serve the business owner, but simply to serve the tax collectors, meaning business owners reluctantly pay accountants to produce them.

That's why, at the moment, so few people really value your role.

Technology is destroying the role of the traditional accountant.

That's why it's time to leave it behind and move on to a new role. A role that uses the skills you've learned and honed over the years, utilises the experience you've gained, and will bring you much higher rewards – both financially and personally.

An opportunity to be seized

As the title of this section suggests, there are three options that immediately spring to my mind:

- Step up – repurpose your skills and make your practice future proof.

- Step out – Sell up.

- Sign on – A consequence of burying your head in the sand.

So let's look at these a little more closely.

One option is to not change anything. Change is always scary and it's certainly easier to carry on doing what you've always done, hoping to get the results you've always got. The problem is that's no longer an option. Times have changed, so you won't get what you've always got. Instead, you'll find you're working much harder and earning less for it.

Take a look back over all the years you've been practicing as an accountant. Have your fees ever really reflected the true value of your skills and experience? Is the life you're living the one you hoped for – or expected – when you decided to become an accountant?

- How many hours per week do you work?

- How many holidays do you get to take? And I don't just mean physically going away somewhere, but a proper relaxing holiday. One where you don't feel the need to have constant access to emails and your phone.

- How much enjoyment and fulfilment do you really get from your work?

Often, when I ask these questions and I'm presented with horrifying answers, I'm given rationalisations such as: "Well, I'm a workaholic. I like working lots of hours and I don't really enjoy relaxing." Even if that's the case though, there's a huge difference between wanting to work lots of hours and having to work them. Which camp are you in?

One reason for working so many hours is that business owners are driving down the fees you can charge for compliance work. They don't value your work because it's not something they particularly want to have done, it's simply something they need to have done. To win work, you're having to undercut your competitors – which in effect means you're working for a pittance and with lots of clients. Basically you've become a production line, processing as many accounts as possible.

This process only cements the fact that the accounts you're working so hard to produce serve no real purpose to the business owner. As you're having to produce these accounts so quickly, you don't have time to look out for great opportunities for your clients, to spot the trends that could lead to success – or disaster – or to bring your experience of other businesses to the table.

At the same time, more and more business clients are becoming aware of one-click accounting solutions. This means either they'll cut out accountants completely and implement the software themselves, or they'll stick with an accountant, but offer ever lower fees because they know that it's a one-click solution.

So, if you're not prepared, all too soon this vicious cycle could put you out of business altogether and have you signing on for benefits...

The best opportunity, however, should you choose to accept it, is one that will bring you a far greater sense of purpose and fulfilment. It will bring much higher financial rewards and allow

you to work fewer hours and to spend more time doing the thi
you really want to – whether that's spending more time with ʾ
family, or pursuing hobbies or other interests. Maybe you could
even find time to start making use of that gym membership!

So, having agreed that you're working too many hours, aren't able
to relax, and that your income doesn't reflect your knowledge,
skills or effort, I'd now like you to think about how many of your
business clients fall in to that same category. And what if you
could change that?

I've got the sign on the wall...

Over the years, I've visited the offices of hundreds of accountants
to carry out one-to-one discussion and coaching sessions. Many
of these offices have a sign on the door that states "Accountancy
and Business Advisory." However, when I ask about the business
advisory services they deliver, the answers range from "Well, we
don't really offer anything and so we're not really consulted," to
"We occasionally give advice around the going rate for, say, a
receptionist." Thankfully, on some occasions, I do actually hear
"We deliver business growth solutions that help the businesses
we work with become more profitable and successful."

Sadly though, I don't hear that last response anywhere near often
enough. And yet there's so much opportunity for accountants to
evolve, to become providers of business growth solutions, and to
complement their skills with numbers. In fact, they have far
more to offer than the typical business consultant or coach,
whose experience is limited to perhaps one or two industries.
Accountants deal with many different industries, they know how
the mechanics of business really work and they already have
trusted relationships with their clients.

Do you want to really make a difference?

Firstly, I'd like you to picture one of your busiest business clients. One who:

- Works countless hours.

- Checks their phone every few minutes for new emails or messages.

- Rarely takes holidays – and certainly not one where they leave their phone at home.

- Struggles with their relationships.

- Is missing their children growing up.

- Is stressed and on edge most – if not all – the time.

Now imagine working with that client. Imagine transforming his or her business so that it works and serves its owner, rather than the other way around. Help them work fewer hours and earn more, help them build a business that allows them to take relaxing, uninterrupted holidays, no checking emails or taking calls, just relaxing whilst their business continues to run and generate their income.

How would that make your client feel? What difference would you have made to their life? You might have:

- Saved a marriage.

- Enabled a parent to be part of their children's lives.

- Extended their life by reducing their stress levels.

What value could they place on that?

That's why this book is not just about earning bigger fees. It's about using your skills with numbers to make a positive difference to the lives of the people you work with. It's only as a consequence of this that you'll be financially, emotionally and spiritually rewarded.

What are you afraid of?

I've worked with enough accountants over the years to appreciate the daunting nature of what I'm describing. Moving from delivering mainly compliance services to offering your services as a business growth expert can seem quite a leap. The only difference really though is that now you'll be delivering a paid-for service rather than the ad-hoc one I suspect you've been giving away free for years.

At this point, I'm sure your heads are buzzing with questions such as:

- Do I really have the skills and knowledge to deliver this kind of service?

- How on earth do I change clients' perceptions that I'm 'just an accountant' – particularly ones I've worked with for a long time?

- How do I position and charge for this service, rather than just deliver advice reactively?

Do keep reading if you'd like to find the answers to these questions – and to many more besides...

Why should people listen to you?

So you're 'just an accountant,' right? And no doubt you've worked with some of your clients for far too long to change their perception of you? In fact, perhaps it would be better to only offer your new service to new clients? WRONG! WRONG! WRONG!

Changing people's perceptions really isn't difficult as long as you use the correct approach. Not only can I teach you what this approach is, but I can also give you some indispensable shortcuts.

To prove it, I'd now like you to take a few minutes to grab a sheet of paper and jot down your key recommendations for a client who fits the following criteria:

A business owner who:

- Works 70 hours per week.

- Has 100 regular customers.

- Earns enough to pay the bills.

- Has £20,000 tied up in current jobs.

- Has £25,000 tied up in debtors.

- Spends far too little time with their children, and whose other personal relationships aren't great either.

My bet is that you didn't take long at all to come up with plenty of suggestions. Suggestions you've probably made to clients before – in passing – that weren't valued precisely because they were delivered in a setting your clients had already labelled 'accounts meeting.'

It's not so much what you say, as how you say it. Many people dislike being told what to do and so reject any ad hoc advice they're given. If it's put to them in the right way, however, they will buy in to it.

That's why making recommendations, then exploring and building on them together, helps business owners see them as their own ideas. Working out the ramifications and quantifying the benefits together will encourage your clients to not only implement your recommendations, but also to see them through.

Positioning yourself as the expert

- Do you write blogs or create videos or podcasts online?

- Do you run regular seminars which your prospective and current clients can attend?

- Have you written a book which you can give to prospective clients as a business card – one with massive impact?

- Do you produce a regular newsletter containing business advice which clients and prospective clients can subscribe to?

- Do you make recommendations during meetings with clients – in a formal way, adding value to the service you deliver?

You'll find that actively producing material in the ways I've just described will jump start making a change to the way you're perceived.

If you're not already doing some – or all – of these, think about clients you've given great advice to in the past. Advice they've implemented which has brought them great results. Could you go back and capture that somehow, perhaps by interviewing them using your phone? Prospective clients need proof that you'll be able to help them, and the best way to do this is through high-quality case studies.

Although this might sound like a Catch 22 situation, one in which you need the proof before you get the work, but you can't get the proof until you've got the work, don't panic. I have a strategy for this too. So, even if you don't have any examples yet, all is not lost. It's never too late to start building your positioning. (Later, in part 4, I'll be giving you some suggestions on how to deliver business growth programmes to your clients, so I'll remind you then how important it is to build a video repertoire of case studies, and the best way to go about this).

Before we continue, I'd like to give you a brief introduction to each of the following sections so you understand what to expect and why I've broken the book down into these five parts.

Part 1. Explains why evolving your role as an accountant is an absolute must. It presents what I believe is the next logical step, and why your skills with numbers lend themselves perfectly to this role.

Part 2. Teaches you how to evolve your role. Using insights and experience I've gained over many years, I'll teach you the best techniques to use – as well as what you need to understand first – to help your client most successfully. (There's a lot of information here, but please don't feel you have to master everything before you start to offer the new service to clients. Having an initial awareness is sufficient – you can build on your skills as you deliver the service). I also share the mnemonic that helps me to provide a structure in my own questioning process: LUKASS.

Part 3. Gives you insights in to the types of topics to cover with your client and gives you ways to help your client improve on those areas, areas that when really focused upon will have a huge positive impact on your client's business.

Part 4. Teaches you how to package, promote and deliver business advisory sessions in a way that not only gets great results for your clients, but also gets great case studies for you, and ensures you're justly rewarded both financially and emotionally.

Part 5. Finally, as products are generally one-off transactions rather than the recurring income you're accustomed to through compliance work, Part 5 explains how to generate recurring income from business advisory services so that you can build up your gross recurring-fee income.

Part 2
Becoming A Sought After Business Advisor

Helping business owners improve their business and, as a direct consequence of this, their lives, is hugely rewarding. In this section I'll share techniques and skills you can use to ensure your sessions with clients are incredibly valuable to them. The techniques needn't be used exclusively in business advisory sessions though. Using them will also help you get the very best out of your team, as well as supporting you in personal situations, whether with children, partners, family or friends.

What you need to know: Your role

Your role is not to know your client's business better than they do. Make it clear that you'll be asking questions to make them reconsider even the most obvious elements of it. I often find that knowing very little about their area leads to the best questions.

It's only when business owners take the time to explain the seemingly obvious stuff in simple terms that they spot the flaws. Be confident about asking them to describe a process in layman's terms.

By asking the right questions and really listening to the answers, your role is to get your clients to consider things differently.

There's a greater chance of buy-in if they're the ones who have developed the idea.

Obtain consent to challenge your clients and to hold them accountable and then do both.

Offer praise. It can be lonely at the top and it's certainly not condescending to say, "Well done. You did a great job there!"

when they've completed an action. Praise and recognition are powerful motivators.

Help them to quantify the impact an action could have and measure its progress. Measure the numbers that matter to your client and keep coming back to these.

Without action what will change?

Action is the key to moving from where you are now to where you want to be. You'd think helping your client come up with a great idea, putting meat on the bones of that idea and turning it into a project with specific next-step actions would be enough for them to transform their business. Sadly, it often takes a lot more than this.

Habits are difficult to break. Most people don't like change and even knowing that what they're doing is detrimental to their health – never mind to their business – won't persuade them to change.

Small changes, however, are easier to swallow than big ones.

Rather than trying to make a big change all in one go, it's easier to make a small one and let that become the norm before making the next.

There's also a huge difference between recognising the need to change and being prepared to make that change. In the section entitled 'Understanding people' on page 51, I'll explain the change journey in more detail and how you can adapt your approach during each stage to help your client progress through the entire journey.

Obtaining consent

People can be very defensive over decisions they've made in the past, even – or particularly – when they know these were the wrong ones, and as a consequence they can sometimes be a little guarded.

Obtaining their consent to challenge and question them, to understand more fully and to hold them accountable encourages them to drop that guard. Examples of ways to do this might include:

- Do you mind if I learn a little more about your business?

- Do you mind if I learn a little more about how your business is affecting your personal life?

- Do you mind if I dig a little deeper?

- Do you mind if I challenge you on that?

You get the idea.

A coach? A mentor? Or a consultant?

I'm sure you've heard all three terms used in connection with helping people and businesses to improve. And often, you'll find, once the role someone is actually playing is described, you'll discover they've been used incorrectly. That's why I'm going to start by giving you my take, and explaining the difference between the three roles. I'll then move on to how to apply and combine each role in the service you deliver, to make sure you achieve the best results for the person you're helping.

What is consulting?

A business consultant is a person with academic qualifications or significant experience in a particular field which they can apply to a business. Examples might include fire and safety consultant, marketing or pricing consultant – not to mention the all-encompassing category 'business consultant' itself.

Now, think back for a moment to the last time you asked for advice. My bet is that this was reactive – you had a particular problem and consulted a professional/expert in that area. A consultant will listen to the particular challenge you face, assess the situation, and provide a set of recommendations – a prescription, if you like – that you can follow to overcome that challenge.

Undoubtedly, consulting has its place. Sometimes we need a prescription – a quick fix we can follow to put right things which are simply not working.

A consultant tells us what we need to do.

What is mentoring?

A mentor is someone who's been there, done that, and got the T-shirt. They've already made a particular journey. They've experienced the pain, overcome the challenges and gained a wealth of experience in the process.

This experience means not only that they're able to relate to your situation, but that they can also suggest great ways to improve it.

They can teach you and train you to think like they do and share the processes which worked for them. Processes you can then apply to your own business and life to achieve similar success to theirs.

A mentor relates, suggests and teaches.

What is coaching?

Coaching, in my view, questions ignorance. Let me explain.
The purpose of pure coaching is getting your client to think for
themselves and to improve their thinking. To help them discover
answers and solutions for themselves.

A coach isn't afraid to ask the obvious questions – questions that
all too often are taken for granted. Or to ask people to explain
why they do what they do and how things could be better.

A good coach won't give or suggest answers. The answer lies
within the coachee themselves, and the coach's role is to ask the
thought-provoking questions that help them get to it. They do
this not by asking leading questions that take the coachee to a
pre-determined answer, but by remaining open in their
questioning, by refusing to cast judgement, and by continuing to
drill down until the coachee develops a solution.

Even if the coach possesses a wealth of knowledge and
experience in this particular area and could easily provide a
solution, they shouldn't. Helping the coachee to discover answers
for themselves develops the coachee and often creates something
unique and innovative from the situation.

That's why I say: A good coach questions ignorance.

Blending the three – but in the right way

All three roles have their place. All three are incredibly
important – but I believe the best approach is to switch from role
to role depending on the situation.

Imagine, for example, that you go to see your doctor because
you're ill. The doctor will assess you by asking a series of
questions and by performing an examination with a view to
getting past your symptoms and understanding their cause. Once
they've done that, they'll give you a prescription. And, if you

follow the course of action they prescribe, your health should return to normal.

However, at this point, imagine your doctor asks to see you again.

This time the visit isn't reactive. Instead, your doctor has requested you see them to discuss your general state of health. Although they've provided the remedy to your previous illness, your habits leave you susceptible to further problems and they'd like to work with you to improve aspects of your health.

Unfortunately, experience suggests that if your doctor gives you a prescription this time you're less likely to follow it. If, for example, you've been a smoker all your life, you don't do much by way of exercise and your diet consists largely of fatty foods, then the outlook isn't great. Simply giving you a prescription that states: 'Stop smoking, eat more of these foods and less of these, and jog around your local park three times per week' won't get much buy in.

At this point your doctor needs to change tack. They need to move towards educating – mentoring – about the impact these habits are having on your health and quality of life. They need to ask the right questions to understand why you have these habits and what you believe are their consequences. Only then can they explore with you what you'd be prepared to change. Even one small change would be great – trying to change too many things or even too much of one thing at once is difficult and wouldn't last anyway. Your doctor would be happy if you simply committed to going for a walk once or twice a week, switched to healthier meals occasionally, or perhaps just smoked fewer cigarettes per day.

Your doctor has switched from being a consultant to being your mentor and coach – albeit one with an ulterior motive. And pure coaching should always be towards a mutually agreed outcome or objective.

When you work with a business owner in a business growth capacity, exactly the same principles apply: What fires are they fighting right now?

When you're in the thick of things it's often difficult to make good decisions. Your clients may well be intelligent and forward-thinking business people, but if they're running around like headless chickens, logical – let alone creative – thinking may be a struggle.

This is where your consulting role comes in. Looking at a situation from the outside often means that you can see a solution that your client simply can't. Alternatively, by helping them to step back a little you could guide them through the process of 'looking in from the outside' and encourage them to think of their own solutions.

Imagine your accountancy practice has its own canteen. (It may well have, of course, but if not, then imagine it does.) One day you're striding down the corridor on your way to an important meeting when, just as you pass the canteen, you spot a fire in the kitchen. As there's a fire extinguisher just inside the door you grab it, put out the fire and everything's good. It's left a bit of a mess, but fortunately you got to it before it caused too much damage. Order is restored and you can carry on to your meeting – a little late but fortunately you have a cast-iron excuse.

The next day, again just as you're heading to an important client meeting, you pass the canteen and exactly the same thing is happening. Once again you grab the extinguisher, put out the fire before it can take hold, things carry on as normal, and you rush off to your client meeting.

In a story, of course, the same thing can happen again and again and again. In real life though, it wouldn't. I doubt you'd even walk away from the fire after the first time without ensuring that the events that led to it were dealt with so that it would never happen again.

And yet...!

In business, metaphorical fires are being put out all the time (accounting firms are no exception, by the way), but the owner is often so busy that they just don't commit the time needed to understand the cause and to put things in place that could prevent the fires in the first place. They – or their team – rush to the rescue, deal with it in the short-term, but then return to whatever they were dealing with before that. Possibly fighting another fire!

I'm sure most business owners are clever enough to put a solution in place for themselves but, because they feel they're in a constant battle, the fear that spending time on just one fire runs the risk of all the others getting out of control.

The reality is often most of the fires share a common cause. And, by working with your client, you can help them to focus on what that cause is and together come up with solutions.

If your client is in a state of panic, it's your role to be calm and decisive (just like the doctor), to be the consultant who asks the questions which drill down to the root cause of those fires, and then to make recommendations on how best to put them out – and prevent them happening again.

Finally, be mindful that each client will respond to each of the three roles differently. Some people prefer to be given clear steps to follow, others will take comfort in knowing that a specific recommendation you're giving has worked for others in their industry and some really don't like to be told how to run their business, but will welcome the thought provoking questions a coach would ask them. I fall in to that latter category...

Personally I'm really grateful to my business coach. In each session, he asks me questions that really make me think about the things I already do, the decisions I'm considering, and my general approach. Although it's good to have a desired outcome for a session, even on the occasions when I don't have a specific problem or idea that I'd like to thrash out, my coach simply asks me general questions. Then, through intense listening, he's able to pick up on the slightest difference in my tone and drill down – knowing there's a problem to be explored. He's usually right –

even if whatever that something is didn't spring to mind when he asked me what I'd like to discuss in the session.

He's great at listening and questioning, which in my view are the most powerful tools you need in order to deliver an effective coaching session.

The LUKASS approach

I use a six-step process when I'm coaching. It takes my clients on a journey from how things are now, to having a clear set of actions that will (if implemented) take them much closer to their desired outcome.

Luckily, this six-step process happens to form a memorable mnemonic: LUKASS. The first four steps are purely about gaining understanding and, until we reach 'Solving,' I never contribute opinions or suggestions.

Having worked with hundreds of accountants over the years, I know that many of them share certain personality traits. One, for example, being caution. While being cautious can be a strength – blindly going into something without considering the risks is always unwise – identifying the risks and only focusing on why it's a bad idea can sometimes mean an idea doesn't get the chance to develop.

There are millions of great ideas out there which never got off the ground because somebody put a dampener on them too soon. Others, no matter how much effort was put in, never came to anything anyway. But some – despite early criticism – went on to change the world.

As an accountant, although you're ideally placed to provide forecasts and to help with business plans, my advice would be to always remain neutral. Provide optimistic, pessimistic and 'somewhere-in-between' forecasts and analysis and then let the entrepreneur make their own decision.

Learn

Tell me about it (a problem/situation/idea).
How does that make you feel?
What are the consequences?
How has that impacted on your business/personal life?

1

Underlying

Use root cause analysis.
What might have led to that happening?
Why would that happen?
What happened just before that?

2

Key Perspectives

If you were your customer/that specific team
member/your partner, what might your perception be?
Put yourself in their shoes.

3

Abracadabra

If you could wave a magic wand, what would be your
ideal outcome?

4

Solving

What are you going to do about that?
Don't Know? If you did know, what would it be?
Brainstorm steps needed to get to the magic wand outcome.

5

Strategy

What are the actions you need to take?
When do each of those actions need to happen by? Why then?
Exercises: Quadrants, 80/20, The Right Questions
What can you do right away to get the ball rolling?

6

In a coaching capacity, however, the LUKASS process will allow
you to play a role in developing ideas, helping your client to
consider possible outcomes and plan for – and around –
challenges.

Let's go through each stage of the LUKASS process and look at
the skills and techniques needed and most utilised at each stage.

Learning

Learning is about listening and asking the right questions in order to ensure that all of the facts, thoughts and details have been ascertained. Largely this section is about enabling your client to vent off over a challenge or to let them air their idea and pour out their thoughts. Your role is to listen and entice the information out.

Although everyone might think they already know how to ask a question, learning how to ask the right questions, and to work out the real answer from your client's response, can be difficult. The purpose of this section is to equip you with the basic skills you need in this area to deliver much more value to the clients you work with.

Questions are the answers

The brain loves being asked a great question. It triggers explosions of synaptic activity in the mind. Asking questions leads to discovery and inventions: "What if I?" "How could I?"

Great questions can lead to you being able to provide more added-value services to your clients. Often, though, this doesn't happen, simply because the wrong question is asked at the end of meetings or other interactions with clients. For example, how often do you ask: "Is there anything else I can help you with?"

The problem is, it's a closed question. One that leads to a "yes" or "no" answer. And something as generic as that most often results in a no. Many people make this mistake when asking for referrals, too: "Do you know anyone who might benefit from my services?" Again, it's a closed question.

In both situations a leading question would be better. Take asking for referrals for instance. If you explain the type of person you'd really like to work with, their mindset, the industry they work in and the size of their company, then a picture will form in the mind of the person you're describing them to. Follow that description with a question such as, "Who do you know who fits that description?" and you're far more likely to get a name. Follow that with, "Who else?" and then again, "Who else?" and you're likely to get three names.

Only use a closed question when you want a yes/no answer. For example: "Are you ready to tackle this situation head on?"

The beauty of asking questions in a coaching capacity is that you don't need to know all the answers. Just the questions.

Although not just any questions, of course. The best questions are those which enable the recipient to really think, to really question and explore a situation, predicament or idea. And there are a few things you need to know about questions first if you're going to get the most out of them...

Questions answered: Context is all

When a close friend asks how you're doing, you might give them an hour's run down on every single thing that's good, bad and ugly right now. Someone else asking though, will probably lead to a different answer. For example:

> *Accountant: How are you doing?*
> *Client: Great thanks. The business is doing okay, although cash flow's a bit tight.*

> *Doctor: How are you doing?*
> *Patient: Well, I keep getting these boils...*

It's important to appreciate this, especially if you've worked with a client in your capacity as an accountant for some time and your main interactions up to now have tended to be pleasantries. If that's the case, the best way to overcome it is by exploring a little further and showing genuine interest: "Tell me more – how are things really doing?" "Are you getting everything you need from your business?" "How are things at home?"

Sometimes, however, you may continue to receive deflective answers, which is something I'll teach you how to deal with in the section entitled 'Underlying' on page 33.

Types of questions

Here's a brief overview of the main types of questions.

Closed questions
I described above a situation in which closed questions can be useful and how using them can encourage a decision – on whether to take action, ascertain whether to explore something, even whether your client is happy for you to challenge them. Usually a closed question results in a short specific answer. For example "When does this need to happen by?"

Open questions
As the description suggests, there's no agenda behind an open question. You're not looking for a specific answer or trying to lead your client down a specific path. You're simply asking something that could lead anywhere. For example "How are you feeling?" could lead to any emotion being described.

Leading questions
In coaching, leading questions should be avoided since they can limit a client's thought processes. For example "How angry does that make you feel?" tends to make a client focus on that one emotion or even amplify it. Assuming that anger is their response to the situation means the questioner is failing to remain neutral and non-judgemental – the client may be feeling more sad or worried than angry. By contrast, the open question I gave above – "How does that make your feel?" – is completely neutral.

Rhetorical questions
A rhetorical question isn't intended to provoke an answer, but a

thought. They're most often used to stimulate an audience's thinking during a public speech or a play.

Are you listening? Or waiting to speak?

"Seek first to understand, then to be understood"
– Stephen R Covey

Questions are incredibly important, but always remember their purpose is to elicit a response from your client. There's an expression, "We have two ears and one mouth and they should be used in that ratio." I'd even argue that it should be more like 50:1.

And I don't mean simply remaining quiet – I mean truly listening. Truly listening takes mental effort. It's not easy and it certainly doesn't come naturally to most of us, but in order to give the best service to your client it's vital.

In Stephen Covey's book, 'The 7 Habits of Highly Effective People', he explains that there are five levels of listening, moving from 'ignoring' through to 'empathic'.

Below, I'd like to share my take on those levels with you.

Level 1. Ignoring
This probably speaks for itself. You're getting on with your work whilst someone is talking to you and you're paying them no attention whatsoever.

Level 2. Glazing over
How many times have you been talking to someone when they've glazed over? They're looking at you – pretending to listen – but you know they're not.

Similarly, how many times has someone been talking to you when you've completely zoned out? Instead of listening, you're thinking about something completely different, whether that's a meeting you've got coming up, wondering how the next match will pan out, or what to do about your leaking roof.

The point is, we know when we're not being listened to. Your client will soon stop sharing anything about their business and personal life if they don't feel that you're interested.

One trigger that can cause people to glaze over is when what's being said differs from their own beliefs and values. However, if you start to judge what's being said then you're not allowing yourself to fully understand the person you're listening to. And, until you fully understand them, you can't discover why their view of the world differs – or seems to – from yours.

Casting judgement also means that your mind has gone off on a tangent. It means that instead of listening, you're having an internal dialogue about the part you did listen to and disagreed with. In all likelihood you've stopped even pretending to listen and are busy arguing or challenging a point in your head – in which case you're definitely not seeking to understand.

Level 3. I'm listening... Oh look – a hot air balloon!
The ears are just one of our senses and it can be difficult to only use our ears without also taking in the smells, sounds and images surrounding us.

It's difficult to spot something interesting behind the person you're trying to listen to without allowing your eyes to shift to it. At a networking event, for example, you might have clocked the next person you want to talk to. Or, during a meeting, you may take a quick glance at the clock or at whoever's just walked past the window.

If you are noticing things in the background then your focus isn't completely on the person you're listening to.

The person you're supposed to be listening to will always notice and – either consciously or unconsciously – realise you're not listening.

Level 4. Formulating

Your inner dialogue is kicking in again. You've listened and heard your client make a point, but they're still talking and now you're eager to give your response. You've had an idea or you've heard something worth drilling down into but – annoyingly! – your client is still talking. So you're waiting for a gap, for him or her to pause for breath, so you can interject, ask your burning question or make that amazing suggestion.

As I've suggested, ego plays a large part in this. You've had a great idea – and it may be genuinely fantastic – and you're keen to convey it. The fact is though that you've stopped listening. Your client may be explaining how they've tried various ideas, or telling you there's an even bigger issue, but you're no longer listening. Instead, you're waiting for a pause.

Level 5. Tunnel focus

The environment around you is no more than a blur as the person you're listening to is the only thing in your sight. You're focused on what they're saying and how they're saying it. This is difficult to do but let me explain why it's so important and a technique to use to do it effectively.

The actual words spoken play a very small part in communication. We derive – or give away – far more from the tone in which they're said and more still from people's facial expressions, hand gestures and stance.

You don't need to be a body language expert. Our subconscious mind is naturally attuned to interpreting these additional elements as long as we remain focused. The emotion behind the words will then come through and allow you to really empathise with clients – and with anyone else you talk to.

Although suppressing your inner dialogue can be difficult, a useful technique is to inwardly repeat every word you hear. Then, when your client has finished talking, use the silence to consider your response. If the silence is awkward there's no harm in explaining that you'd like a minute to think about what they've been saying.

This demonstrates that you've really listened. You may have spotted a shift in body language, for example, or you may have been intrigued by something in particular that was said. If so, write this down – along with any other points that come to you – and then decide which you're going to explore first.

For me, a change in body language (a shift in the position of their body, for example) can suggest a deeper emotion behind what's being said. (Although never assume this – they may just have become uncomfortable from sitting too long in one position!) To find out, I'd suggest you simply paraphrase the relevant point back to them, asking them to explain a little more or even directly asking: "Is there more to this than you said?"

Underlying – Drilling down past the symptoms to the cause

It's vital to listen (Level 5) and to observe your client while they're answering your questions.

Really focusing on what someone is saying, on their tone and body language, will help you identify which areas to drill down into. However, I don't expect you to be an instant body-language expert – being consciously focused is often all it takes to spot the obvious.

If someone mentions a subject that bothers them, for example, their tone will change or, owing to the discomfort it causes them, they might shift their body position. If you see this happen it's always worth asking them to "Tell me more about..." honing in on the word they used.

Earlier, using the example of an accountant and a doctor asking the same question, I mentioned how sometimes people tell you only what they assume you want to hear. Quite often, in fact, people will give a superficial answer to questions and it's your job to show genuine interest by digging further and really getting to understand the situation.

In addition, different people have different personalities. Some will talk endlessly about anything – my nine year old son is a perfect example! – while others tend to talk in bullet points, simply giving one-sentence answers, or even less.

Here, then, are a couple of techniques to get people to open up a little.

The most important is always to show genuine interest. Ask an open question and remain silent while they answer. Then, if you haven't received much of an answer, ascertain why. Do they feel it's none of your business? Or perhaps they're simply in a rush – particularly if you ask your question off the cuff rather than during a dedicated meeting. But you won't know this unless you ask. For example "Do you mind me understanding a little more about that?"

If there's a genuine reason why now isn't a good time, they'll tell you. And, if they do, you could follow up by explaining that you'd love to better understand so perhaps next time... In my experience, people's response to that tends to be okay. And then – because you've shown you're genuinely interested – their guard begins to relax. Gaining consent is important, and something I'll address more specifically later.

However, once your client becomes more open and starts to give much lengthier answers, it's still important to really listen and observe because long answers from one person don't always reveal much more than short ones from someone else.

A good tip is to listen to their answer and then, once they've stopped talking, simply nod in acknowledgement and raise your eyebrows slightly as though you're waiting for more information. In fact, do this a couple of times. It may be uncomfortable at first – there may even be a stunned silence – but make sure you're not the one to fill it. Instead, wait for them to say something, even if this sometimes takes many seconds and those seconds feel like minutes. If ever you feel really uncomfortable, you can always simply say: "Tell me more about that."

Sometimes, of course, you may get another short sentence in response. In which case, repeat the whole procedure again. If it still doesn't work, then try picking up on a word they've used by asking, "What do you mean by [that word]?"

The purpose of this exercise is to dig through their superficial answer and hone in on anything which seems to cause them discomfort.

Another response you might get to a question such as, "Tell me, are you enjoying your business right now?" (and yes, I know it's a closed question, but I find it's a great way to make people think about whether or not they really are enjoying it) is, "Yes, it's great thanks." If so, then ask them to tell you more. What's doing well? Show genuine interest and let them talk you through it. Once they've explained, say something like, "That sounds fantastic. I'm really pleased. Although of course, every business comes with its fair share of challenges, too. What challenges are you facing right now?"

Always ask "Why?"

"Why?" is the most powerful question of all.

It forms part of the drilling down exercise I talked about earlier, when I explained that often the first response you get to a question is superficial. In fact, often you need to work through many layers before you get to the real answer.

Always use your judgement as to when you need to drill down, but getting someone to really think about why they do – or plan to do – something is important. Are they doing it for the right reasons? Sometimes it's simply because they've always done it that way, other times it might be because they're out to please or impress someone. A carefully timed "Why?" has the power to make them stop and think.

The following story has been circulating on the Internet for years. I use it in my coaching sessions as a great example of people doing something just because it's always been done that way.

A woman is making dinner for her boyfriend for the first time and decides to try her hand at her mother's brisket recipe, which includes cutting off the ends of the roast the way her mother always did. Her boyfriend says it's delicious, but asks "Why do you cut off the ends – that's the best part!" She answers, "That's the way my mother always makes it."

The next week, they go to her mother's house for dinner, and her mother prepares her famous brisket recipe, similarly cutting off the ends. The daughter is sure she must be missing some vital information, so she asks her mother why. And her mother answers, "That's the way my mother always makes it."

The next week, to get to the bottom of it, all three of them visit the girl's grandmother, and her grandmother says, "That's the only way it'll fit in my old pan!"

Key perspectives

Sometimes, particularly when we're too emotionally close to a situation, it's hard to imagine a different outcome or to come up with new ideas. If that's the case, I find it incredibly useful to get the people I'm coaching to do one – or more – of the following.

- Put themselves in their customers' shoes.

- Put themselves in a particular team member's shoes.

- Have an out of body experience!

Remember, no matter how thinly you slice a cake there are always two sides.

Many years ago, for example, I was involved in a dispute with an associate of my company with whom we had a commercial arrangement to generate business. A few years in, however, we learned that for some time he'd also been happily benefiting – to the tune of several hundred thousand pounds – from a different arrangement with an independent business with whom we also had an arrangement. He was receiving a commission as an introducer, he was in fact never an introducer and the commission fee he had been receiving was our entitlement.

The Board of Directors and the shareholders were understandably annoyed and decided to take legal action. Although I was one of those Directors and shared the general annoyance, I wanted to understand how the situation had arisen. So I put myself in our associate's shoes and went back to the beginning of our relationship with him – where I realised a simple misunderstanding had led to his benefitting to the extent he had.

Analysing things in this way allowed me to discover the initial cause of the problem and to address it. Yes, we still took legal action, but instead of focusing solely on that, we got to the root cause and made sure it couldn't happen again.

Putting yourself in someone else's shoes enables you to see things from a different perspective.

So, if your client is frustrated over a disagreement with one of their customers, suggest they put themselves in that customer's shoes while you talk them through what the customer might be feeling. Take them right back to before the disagreement began, reliving it from the customer's perspective. It may help them to see the situation in a new light, or even to come up with a win-win solution.

This is partly what I meant by 'have an out of body experience.'

I'm sure you can relate to the fact that it's far easier to give someone advice on improving their business than it is your own. This is because we're often too close to our own business, and too close to the problem surrounding us. A question I often ask clients is "If you were able to step outside your own body, leaving all your emotions behind, and to look at yourself from the other side of the room, what would you be telling yourself right now?"

I've found that's a question which unlocks doors. Seeing things from a disconnected state allows different parts of the brain to kick in, which in turn leads to new ideas.

Do a little exercise yourself right now and imagine you're a prospect who's never set foot in your office before. What do you see – and think – when you walk into your office, looking at it from this different perspective? Because you walk in there every day, you probably no longer notice the things that a fresh pair of eyes might see. Does it look old or modern? Do the walls need a fresh coat of paint? What does it smell like? When prospects arrive, are they made to feel welcome? What's their overall impression when they visit for the first time?

The first half of the LUKASS process is about teasing as much information out of them as possible, specifically drilling down to the root cause (of the problem) and/or reason why they've come up with a great idea. Now, with all of that information in mind, the second half of the LUKASS process is around idea generation and then formulating a plan of action.

Abracadabra

Now that we've progressed through the first half of the LUKASS process we're now in the realms of idea generation. However, the most important ideas to explore are the ones which come from your client and we're not done with listening and asking questions yet.

Often we try and plot out a route from where we are now to where we want to be and because there's often baggage; existing problems and challenges, we work with those in mind and struggle to see a great outcome as a result.

Asking your client if they could wave a magic wand... or if anything were possible... can often lead to a different kind of outcome to a problem that's been aired or an idea that needs to be implemented. It provides new ground for exploration, removing the mental blocks of reality. Sometimes tapping in to magic means tapping in to our creativity, and even if the magic wand solution is impractical it can get the juices flowing.

Actively encourage the implausible. Let your client really go to town on their magic wand solution. This creates new routes around or right through the mental obstacles to the possibilities.

Be mindful that the creative side of the brain functions much more slowly than the logical side. Creativity is often lost because people lose their patience and move on before the creative side of the brain has had a chance to do its job. The logical side of the brain is the cause of the impatience, it functions incredibly quickly. The creative side of the brain works in pictures and objects. These have to be unraveled and processed.

I won't get too technical about how the brain functions except to say exercise patience and encourage the magic wand solution.

Solving: Adopt the right mind set

When I was about nine years old, after a great day out at Hathersage in the UK's Peak District with my auntie and uncle, we returned to their house for dinner. Whilst we were awaiting it, my sister and I were sitting in their living room watching TV when suddenly, beneath the TV, I saw a computer. (Remember, this was the early 80s and at this point I'd never seen one before).

My uncle was studying computer programming at university and, as I was so intrigued, he was happy to switch it on and let me take a look. Although it didn't have any games, and essentially all that happened was a flashing cursor appeared on the screen, he did type a few bits of code in to show me how you could create a simple programme.

A few days later, when I got home from school I saw my uncle's car parked outside. He'd decided to purchase a better computer for himself and to let me have his old one. He sat down with me whilst we connected it to the living room TV and switched it on. Again I was presented with a flashing cursor and nothing else.

At that point he handed me a very thick book; one which contained many examples of code, and suggested I type one while he went for a cup of tea with my parents. When I'd finished, I told him and he came and sat beside me on the floor as we typed in "RUN" and hit return. Although we were then presented with the words "SYNTAX ERROR" – there were typos in my code – we went through and corrected it together and several attempts later it ran!

The code I'd used simulated – in the most basic manner – a fruit machine. It presented three symbols on the screen, you hit the space bar and it randomly generated three new symbols. If they matched, a message appeared saying "WELL DONE." If they didn't, it said "TRY AGAIN."

It was a very basic game, but it took a tremendous amount of code to create it.

My uncle then said something I found confusing, telling me "You don't really need all that code to achieve the same game." I vividly remember not understanding his statement. "Surely," I thought, "Surely a computer needs every one of those commands to do what it just did – otherwise it wouldn't work in the same way."

However, he proceeded to erase all my code and start again. I watched as he typed about a quarter of the amount of code I'd copied from the book and then ran it. And he was right. It worked! It did exactly the same as before but with much less code. So, as my uncle had discovered, there's always a better way – you just need to use your brain a bit more.

That concept stuck with me and became my mindset. Although not one – "Is there a better way?" – I'd ever use as a question. As I said, it's a mindset. There IS always a better way, and I apply that thinking to everything I do.

Every time I observe a system, a process, or a way that something is done I do so with that mindset, looking to simplify the steps and achieve the same or even a better outcome. In everything we do, whether in our business or in our personal life, we effectively follow a system – a series of commands much like that of the computer. Take something as apparently simple as making a cup of tea, for example. It's a system we subconsciously follow:

Step 1. Check water in kettle. If low, fill it to required level.

Step 2. Switch on kettle.

Step 3. Whilst kettle is coming to boil, prepare the teapot...

And so on.

I've learned that every process can be simplified and I've applied that thinking to every system I've looked at in businesses. Sometimes I might design software programmes to automate processes and at other times I might help to identify a more effective, streamlined and efficient way of achieving the same – or a better – outcome.

I strongly believe that anyone who takes on my attitude – the mindset that there is always a better way – would achieve the same outcomes.

And that's the reason for my story, and for the heading to this section of the book: I implore you to adopt this same mindset, especially during your coaching sessions.

Often when I question someone about one of their systems in a manner that suggests there might be a better method, it triggers something. Because they sense that I know a better way, their brain steps up a gear. It's as if their brain has accepted the challenge to find what I've found.

So, whenever you're exploring possibilities with a client, do so with confidence that there's a better way and make them feel that you're moving towards discovering it together.

Don't recommend – yet! Explore the answer first

As an accountant, you've probably worked with many, many different businesses in many different industries. Chances are, the problem your client is articulating is something you've seen other businesses overcome and, as you know exactly what they did, you're bursting to share this with your client.

The problem is that your client will most likely dismiss your suggestion – for any number of reasons they express verbally. Ultimately, though, they'll have dismissed it simply because it wasn't their idea.

And, what's almost worse, even if they do decide to implement it, you've missed the opportunity to help them develop personally by finding the answer for themselves.

So please remember never to jump straight to a consulting role unless you feel it's really necessary. Instead, use the coaching technique and help your client to develop by asking open questions until they come up with their own solution. One that might be even better than the one you had in mind.

Although, as I've explained, I'm not a fan of asking leading questions, sometimes you might deem it necessary. Let's say, for example, you're working with a roofing business, focusing on how they might attract more customers.

Your questioning might start like this:

You: "How many neighbours of customers approach you during – or just after – a job to ask you about their roof?"

Client: "Not that many, actually."

You: "Let's explore some reasons for that. It may just be that they don't need their roof doing, but if someone did and they saw your people working, what methods could we use to improve the likelihood of them wanting to use your company?"

However, although you go on to explore together ways this could be done, and some great suggestions surface, you've seen the team your client employs. They're incredibly untidy, and one of the supervisors walks around in a vest that doesn't entirely cover his beer belly and is stained with sweat and tomato sauce from his daily bacon sandwich.

If you jump straight in suggesting your client gets his employees to tidy up their appearance, as doing so might get the neighbours more interested in using his company, don't be surprised if he gets a little defensive.

Instead, if your client seems to have run out of ideas, you could try offering a few prompts. Questions such as, "What do the neighbours see when your team's working?" Or "What do you think their opinion of your team might be?"

By using the word "see," you can lead your client to focus on the visual, to use this to filter his or her ideas. And, at this point, you may well find they come up with ideas around putting a sign with their contact details up, or writing their company's name on their vans.

However, if they still fail to mention the appearance of their team, a more specific question about how this might make potential customers see their company may be in order. But only after you've spent considerable time exploring all the other routes, and many other good ideas have surfaced.

As I said, I'm not usually a fan of leading questions. The role I'm encouraging you to take, however, isn't that of a pure coach. Instead, I'm explaining the difference between coaching, mentoring and consulting so that you can use your judgement about which is most suitable at any given moment.

Brainstorming

Brainstorming is an essential part of generating ideas to solve problems and questions form an integral part of brainstorming.

Brainstorming is often not carried out effectively and this has begun to give it a reputation as inept. If done properly though it can lead to some great ideas.

That's why, when I lead a session, I use a six-step formula I learned from David Allen's book, 'Getting Things Done', albeit with a slight adaptation to include Step Five, 'Critique.' Research shows that when ideas are critiqued and challenged with a view to overcoming the flaws together, the ideas are strengthened and further ideas flow from the exercise too. I'll run through the steps with you now.

1. What's the purpose?
Is it to identify the steps needed to complete a project, for example? Or is it to come up with ideas to overcome a particular challenge? Define the purpose of your brainstorming session succinctly and do so in the past tense so that it reads as if the outcome has already been met. For example: "Produced a list of the top ten benefits our latest product – [name of product] – has that makes it so wonderful."

2. What are the rules?
Are there any suggestions that won't be entertained? If so, list them. For example: "Every statement must be supported by evidence."

3. Share your vision
Whether it's for a small project, or a 'big picture' for the business as a whole, articulate it to the group. If it's just you and your client it's still worth articulating. Describe what it might look, feel and sound like. (Even what it might taste and smell like, if applicable). When does it need to be completed? How will you know when it is? Encourage the participant(s) to write down any ideas they have while you talk – often we think of things whilst we're listening, but our brains tend to believe that once they've

presented an idea to our conscious mind, they've done their job. If we don't write this down, the conscious mind suddenly goes blank when the brainstorming begins and the thought is lost.

4. Brainstorm
Only once you've shared the purpose, rules and vision should the actual brainstorming take place. Don't try to focus on chronological structure or to dismiss detail in favour of the big picture. Anything that's raised should be logged, regardless of how small, and with no judgement cast as to its pertinence or discussion allowed. If a particular suggestion triggers a thought, log that too. Allocate a specific amount of time to this – I recommend not more than 10 minutes – set your smartphone to count down, and put it on display.

In terms of logging there are two main methods. You can either keep everyone silent while they write down as many ideas as possible on Post-it notes or into their laptop. (If you're looking for specific software for this, I've used Basecamp, but there are many other options available). The alternative is to have one person noting ideas as everyone else shouts them out. Although this sometimes creates a bottleneck of ideas, the upside is that one person's suggestion can spark an idea from somebody else.

My personal preference is to combine the two. For the first half of the session ask people to be silent while they log their ideas. Then, in the second half, everyone can reel off what they've written. I've also found this method is the most successful at accommodating both extroverts and introverts. (Further information about introverts and extroverts on page 62).

5. Critique
Once you've got your list, encourage people to be critical, to identify flaws in the ideas raised but not with the objective of dismissing them, but of developing them so that they become stronger. (It's also likely that you'll find this process will trigger additional ideas.)

6. Organisation
Reorder the ideas in a logical fashion and discuss which are

necessary. Are there any gaps? If so, what are they? Are the items actions or outcomes? A useful rule of thumb is that when you look at an action you know exactly what you need to do. If it's not that simple it's probably a project or an outcome, which means you'll need to break it down into actions. (Many people add an item to their to-do list but, when they get to it, their eyes glaze over. This often happens when the item they've listed is a project rather than an action, so help your client by ensuring that all actions listed are actions).

"What else?" vs "Anything else?"

This is the final questioning technique I want to share with you. And, since appreciating the difference between the two, I've cringed whenever I've heard the wrong one being asked.

I'm sure you remember my example about referrals, and how "Anything else?" is a closed question. It doesn't provoke a new idea, it doesn't tease the brain into being creative. It simply asks a straightforward question that results in nothing more than a "yes" or "no." And for that reason the answer is most likely going to be "no."

So how about asking "What else?" Well, that's very different. "What else?" suggests there is something else. It challenges your client's brain to come up with the answer it thinks you've already found. And asking it with the mindset I explained above gives your question an air of confidence. I promise you, it's a great technique.

Bring it back to the numbers

As an accountant you already know the impact numbers can have.

Saying, "I can work with you to improve your business and make your life better" doesn't mean anything.

Saying, "I can work with you to enable you to shift from working 70 hours per week to 25 and take your personal earnings from £75K to £150K in the process," definitely does!

Likewise, whenever you're discussing ideas with a client, explore the impact of each on the numbers that matter (I cover this on page 74). How it will impact on profit for example, or on their hours or debtor days etc.

Don't just look at whether it will make the numbers generally better or worse but ascertain its specific impact: "By implementing this system you'll be able to work half an hour less per day," for example.

With numbers, first extrapolate and then condense them: "If we extrapolate that up, half an hour per day equates to three weeks a year you'll be saving." Or "By implementing this idea your profits could increase by £12K per year. Over a 20-year period that would raise £240K in additional income, or give you an additional £1000 per month to spend."

Next, take this further: "What would you do with an extra three weeks per year?" "What would you do with an additional £1000 per month?" Or "What would you do with an additional £240,000 in your bank account in 20 years' time?"

Seeing the actual numbers that could result makes an idea seem more real. It encourages action to be taken to get those benefits. Enhance that by encouraging your client to imagine the bigger picture, by asking them what they could do with those numbers, and their emotional response will almost guarantee action.

Sometimes, you'll find the numbers will be easy to figure out – especially for an accountant. However, as predictions can never be totally accurate, make sure you use phrases such as "potentially achieve profits of…" and never just stick with one idea.

For other predictions, though, it won't be so easy. How do you put a number against something like 'happiness,' for example? Remember, happiness is a feeling and so applying a scale to that feeling is fine. "On a scale of 1 to 10 – where 1 is just wanting to walk away and get a minimum wage job, and 10 is springing out of bed every morning eager to get to work – how happy are you right now with your business?"

With feelings, it's also important to complement the number with a more detailed explanation and to note this down. Happiness, for example, is always relative to a specific time and situation, so be sure to ascertain exactly what it is that's causing their score.

You: On a scale of 1 to 10 – where 1 is just wanting to walk away and get a minimum wage job, and 10 is springing out of bed every morning eager to get to work – how happy are you right now with your business?

Client: Right now it's a 3.

You: Okay, tell me why it's a 3.

Client: I'm working 60 hours a week and I'm getting stressed about it. I'm running around like a headless chicken and there doesn't seem to be any end to the madness in sight. The only reason I can't walk away is because we need the income to pay the bills but, right now, I have no life.

Later, after exploring some possible solutions, come back to this conversation.

You: Now we've explored these ideas, how do you see them impacting on the hours you're working per week?

Client: It seems like they could save me a massive amount of time.

You: And how would that impact on your level of happiness?

Client: I expect it would increase it to at least a 5 – which is a start.

Likewise, in future sessions, go through the tangibles first, the things they've told you were causing their lack of happiness, and then ascertain their happiness scale. This may still be low, but for a different set of reasons. That's why it's important to clarify that the original cause of their unhappiness has been rectified.

It may be, for example, that their happiness level was low initially because they were working too hard and couldn't find a way to reduce this. Later, it may be that they have a problem employee they need to deal with. Both scores may result in a 3, but for very different reasons.

Quantify the benefits

For every single idea or recommendation make sure you quantify the potential benefits. (Remember the 'Bring it back to the numbers that matter' section)? Say you examine how to increase sales by 1-2%. If so, then make sure you calculate and extrapolate that (and not just for the current year but over a five-year period). Similarly, if you work out how to save your client half an hour per day, do the same. Then ask how they'll spend that time, or invest those additional earnings.

Always record the potential benefits and include these when discussing the actions to be taken.

Strategy: When would "now" be a good time?

This has become a catchphrase of mine.

Although we come up with ideas all the time, we rarely implement them. Instead, they get shelved for tomorrow – a tomorrow which never comes.

During sessions make sure you capture any ideas that come up. Then, toward the end of each one, go over these with your client and decide which should be implemented, when and by whom.

Agree which of the ideas are projects that need to be broken down into actions and which are actions that can be carried out immediately.

Set a date against each action. Ask clients if you can hold them accountable and nag them if necessary. (They're likely to say yes but, if they don't, honour this. If, by your next visit, they haven't achieved any of their actions, ask them again. They may well agree this time).

Deadlines, and absolute clarity to avoid any misunderstanding on exactly what needs to be done to complete each action, are crucial.

Once you've agreed the actions, type them up together into a cloud-based project management tool such as Basecamp or Trello. Trello is particularly good as it allows you to create and share access to a project with your client. This means not only can you track their progress but, if they miss a deadline on an agreed action, you can immediately pick up the phone. (Not only will your speed stun them, but if something's come up which means they're having to firefight again, you can help them overcome it).

If you'd like to learn more, or access some additional ideas and exercises, go to: **www.improveyourpractice.co.uk**

That's how the LUKASS process disciplines me when I'm coaching accountants. It helps me ensure that I've learned as much information as I can and I've really drilled down before exploring ideas together. Practice this with your family and friends and see what difference it makes in your communications. People really appreciate being understood. On the subject of people, let's explore them a little further.

Understanding people

"There's nowt as queer as folk" – old Yorkshire expression

The change journey

Change is difficult for anybody, change leads to uncertainty and discomfort. Some people embrace change better than others but it's still not an easy process. Below is a brief description of the six stages of the change journey. It's useful to be aware of these because as a business advisor it's important to recognise where your client is on this journey and adapt your approach accordingly.

Now let's go through these stages in more detail and look at what you can do to help your clients progress to the next stage.

As I describe each stage I make references to different parts of this book. There's no need to go jumping around the book though, I'm merely providing comfort that this book gives you the techniques and the skills required to help your client through every stage.

1. Unaware
The first stage is interesting, isn't it? You've probably heard the analogy of the frog that when placed in hot water will jump straight out, whereas the frog whose watery environment heats up gradually doesn't realise how bad things are getting until it's too late. It's exactly the same for your clients. Often they've always worked long stressful hours and it's become the norm, or things have gradually got worse and worse, but they haven't had time to stop and think about it.

In Part 3 we'll explore a process called 'What are the numbers that matter' on page 74. This is a great tool for taking a client through the process of unaware to recognition.

Or, if you're able to access our BenchMark product, show them

The change journey

Unaware
No recognition that a problem exists, so no apparent need for change.
1

Recognition
Aware of the problem and may even evaluate it. At this point, however, no commitment to action.
2

Prepared
A big step forward from recognition. They're beginning to make small changes, so it's important to help them set larger goals and work out priorities.
3

Committed
Making large changes. On a real mission to make things happen.
4

Accommodating
Sometimes to make the original changes stick, changes to other aspects of their business or life are also necessary. Without this step they could face a setback.
5

Evaluation
Are things better now? Are they likely to get better? It's easy to slip back into old ways if the situation hasn't improved or doesn't seem likely to.
6

how they compare to others in their industry. (Our BenchMark product can be trialled at **www.improveyourpractice.co.uk**). BenchMark allows you to enter data both from the accounts and additional information about the client's business. This data is entered back office at the point of finalising the accounts. The data entered is compared against the thousands of entries for other identical businesses and a report is produced showing how the numbers stack up against the competition. It shows where your client is stronger and weaker. The reason this is such a powerful tool is because many business owners form the assumption that 'this is just the way it is in my kind of business.' For example, long debtor days. Showing them that their direct competition has a much healthier number against that metric can encourage them to accept that things can be better.

By performing either of these exercises you're able to open their eyes to the fact that what they're doing doesn't fit with their ambitions and that something needs to change. However, as I mentioned earlier, there's a big difference between recognising the need for change and being prepared to make that change.

At this point we've simply moved them from unaware to recognition.

2. Recognition

Sadly, many people remain in this recognition stage and never progress to the next level. Take smokers or the overweight for example. Many people know things are wrong but don't take action to prevent it. Sometimes this is because logically they know it's wrong to keep eating fast food and not enough healthy food for example but emotionally, irrationally the fast food tastes better.

Unfortunately our emotions out-rank our logical in the decision making in our brains and throw the internal (and sometimes external) tantrums. Emotions come from the limbic region of the brain which is by far the most primitive and still the most dominant. Getting the limbic region on board with change is necessary.

If you've used the BenchMark product that's available on my website or if you've taken your client through the numbers that matter exercise it's not enough to simply identify the gap between what the numbers could or should be and where they are now. Numbers are merely logical, these are accepted by the logical part of the brain but not the irrational/emotional limbic region.

They'll need to buy in to the need for change emotionally as well as rationally.

The limbic region of the brain is, as I mentioned, very primitive. It's emotion based. It likes to feel good and doesn't like not to. That's the key to helping someone make change.

Connect the numbers on the BenchMark report or the numbers they've come up with on the numbers that matter exercise to their emotions. For example, on the BenchMark report it may show that their gross profits are low compared to the competition. So what? So explore with them that if that number was greater, clearly meaning more income for them, what might they do with that additional income? Do the math with them and show them the cash that might ultimately end up in their back pocket and then take it to the emotional stage. What would you spend that on? When did you last take your family away on holiday. Extrapolate it too, that additional income over five years would be X. What would that mean for you?

Tap in to how their life currently is. Perhaps it's less about the money and more about the hours they're working and how little time they get to spend with family. Perhaps improving the financial numbers would lead to employing others and freeing up their time.

Identify the 'pain' of the current situation and the potential pain of the future if things don't change now. How long can the long hours be sustained for until it puts strain on relationships? Are they spending enough time with their children? Children grow up incredibly quickly and many people regret not spending more time with their children. That's an opportunity that once missed is lost. Yes, they may have more children and do it differently next time, but they can't go back and spend more time with their existing children when it's too late. This is highlighting the pain of the current situation.

The limbic region is very motivated to move away from pain.

Next focus on more on the gain. Help them paint the picture of what life would be like if they worked less hours, came home stress free and were able to switch off from work and fully be there, be in the moment with their family. Ideally, identify their dreams.

This is essential for helping people become prepared for change.

3. Prepared
Your client will now be willing to try making some small changes.

To help them gain confidence in the process, focus on quick wins; low effort, high impact and show them the possibilities.

Use some of the examples from my sales growth drivers chapter entitled 'Getting – and getting more from – customers' on page 84 to ask what they believe the impact might be – in percentage improvements – in each broken-down area. As each of these is intended to generate more income, ask how they'd like to invest this. This opens up even more possibilities and reinforces the need for change.

If long hours rather than income are the problem, focus on the pricing for maximum profit growth driver; help them earn more and at the same time, work with fewer customers. Also focus on the bigger picture. Explore some of the benefits of prioritising and systemising together.

The beauty of these techniques is that they're simple and yet incredibly effective. Small changes leading to pretty big financial results for the business, which can either be invested back in to the business or simply enjoyed.

4. Committed
Once your client has begun to see the positive results of implementing the quick wins they'll be ready to commit to bigger goals and objectives, setting deadlines and formulating action plans that will plough through the changes necessary.

5. Accommodating
As changes in one area of business (or life) begin to happen they affect other areas which also have to change in some way to accommodate these changes. This can begin to overwhelm the person going through the changes, a domino effect is literally happening and so it's important to maintain regular contact and have regular sessions with your client to help keep them on track and focused.

6. Evaluation
Is it working? It's important to measure the progress along the way, as most often with change things get worse before they get

better. Often, as things get worse, people feel that they need to revert back to the old ways because it was better then. This is called the loser trap. Set the expectation with your client that things will likely get worse before they get better. Reassure them along the way and keep measuring the progress.

Part 4 walks you through the process of taking a client through from being unaware of the need to change to being prepared and committed. This will help you promote and deliver a consulting session. That in itself is a consulting session and one that you should deliver at no fee. Once your client recognises the need for change and is prepared to make some changes they'll be willing to work with you on a paid basis.

Change is still difficult, being aware of the loser trap is important and being the support and the 'rock' for your client is too.

Change is unsettling for everybody, different people respond better than others to it and different people also require a different type of support than others. Having a better understanding of behavioural characteristics will help you adapt your approach.

Personal DISC profile

For thousands of years people have been trying to understand each other. In 1928, William Moulton Marston wrote a book called 'The Emotions of Normal People'. He discovered that although we all have very different personalities, made up by our unique experiences, values and beliefs, deep down there are many characteristics which are common to us all. He discovered that these characteristics fell in to four main areas.

- Dominance (D)

- Influence (I)

- Steadiness (S)

- Compliance (C)

Each area forms a heading for a group of characteristics, and each characteristic offers a sliding scale of intensity ranging from one extreme to the other. For example, under Dominance we might range anywhere from Highly Dominant to Highly Submissive.

Although the four areas cannot offer a complete personality analysis, having a knowledge of them helps you understand what motivates and drives people (not everyone is driven by financial incentives, in fact only a few are); how best to communicate with each type of person (technical or big picture) and the type of work they might be best at (leadership or sales etc). It's even possible to identify when frustration is present and the type of frustration.

I've used this type of personal profiling since 2008. It's been useful in many situations – from making sure I recruit the right person, through to regularly profiling teams to reveal any frustrations or spark discussion and profiling customers so that our approach and language is tailored to each individual.

It's a huge subject in itself, so I won't go in to too much detail here, but it's important to appreciate that not everyone can take on similar functions.

To ascertain someone's profile there are online questionnaires that the individual can complete. A graph and report are produced as a result.

Below are a couple of brief examples.

High Dominance

- Goal-oriented and self-driven. Avoids failure at all costs – will happily work long hours and be incredibly resourceful to get jobs done.

- Unchallenged, may become bored and stir up trouble.

- Not keen on detailed work, but will do it if necessary and as long as it's not repetitive or constant.

- Outspoken and critical of those who don't meet their standards. Often hurts or upsets people without knowing. Can be explosive, but doesn't hold grudges.

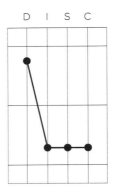

- Also not 'people people,' but remain positive in antagonistic environments.

- Once a project's challenge is over, prefers to leave the finishing off to others.

High Influence

- Hates detail.

- Incredibly positive – tends to get on with anyone and everyone.

- Makes decisions based on summary analysis.

- 'People people,' great at motivating and persuading others.

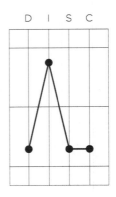

- Loves to help others achieve their objectives – as such may fall behind on their own.

- Motivated by public recognition – likely to display trophies and awards.

- Strives to avoid rejection.

High Steadiness – Completer-finishers

- Patient, kind and amiable. Great listeners with a natural desire to help others.

- If upset, tend to conceal it. If their frustration builds sufficiently, explosive. Can hold grudges.

- Resistant to change, striving to maintain the status quo.

- Family- and team-oriented. Uncomfortable away from their families.

- Forms close-knit groups and strong bonds. Works best as part of a team and are good organisers.

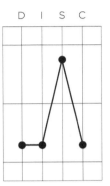

High Compliance – Task oriented

- Technically minded, requiring and gathering lots of information in order to take on a task or make a decision.

- Tends to be perfectionist, a great strength as long as it doesn't slow down a project.

- Always operates within standard procedures because rules are important to them.

- Good at research – likes detail and wants everything they do to be 100% correct.

- Naturally cautious.

- Don't tend to be 'people people,' but loyal and adaptable – particularly in order to avoid conflict.

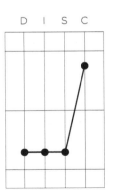

You may relate to one of these descriptions, you may in fact relate to many or even all of them. In different environments we can switch to any of these different profiles. What we're looking for here is the preferred work profile.

I've described just a few characteristics of each of those four categories. Many people will be a combination of one, two, or three of those categories where the dot on the graph is positioned above that central line, and so a person might display a blend of the descriptions. However, they will be most prominent in one of them (whichever is highest). As well as being high (above that centre line) in a category at least one factor and up to three should be below that centre line too as these are supporting factors.

Being below the line shouldn't be taken as evidence of weakness, but as a sign of possessing a different set of strengths. The attributes of people who are low on a scale aren't as outwardly obvious. A Low Influence person, for example, tends to be reserved, reflecting on information they're given rather than rushing to make a decision straightaway. Similarly, a Low Dominance person tends to be much more accommodating, hesitating to make a decision unless it's in an area of their expertise.

Each of us has a blend of these attributes that can be illustrated on a graph. The one shown right, for example, shows an individual's profile of High S and C with Low D and I. The further upward from the centre line an attribute scores, the more prominently it will be displayed by the person.

Understanding people's strengths and playing to them will always get results. Giving a task that requires the characteristics of someone with High Dominance attributes to a High Steadiness person is likely to lead to frustration for the delegator, and discomfort and even, perhaps, inability on the part of the individual.

An effective team, be it a project team or a Board of Directors needs to be comprised of all four types if it is to function most successfully.

The way a task is delegated should also differ according to the profile of who it's delegated to. Whereas a High Compliance person will require lots of detail, a High Influence one won't thank you for it. Similarly, if a High Influence person is delegating to a High Compliance one, they may not provide all the information the latter needs to feel confident in their role.

In a coaching session, this is why I suggest that – for each action or project that comes up with a client – you help them ascertain which of their team is best suited to it. If it's detailed work, for example, do they have someone who is highly compliance? (Although don't forget that if deadlines are tight, a highly compliant individual might find the pressure too much, whereas a high dominant individual would relish the challenge).

Understanding what people are incentivised by – be it financial reward, public recognition or simply having extra time to spend with their family – will also help clients get the best from their team.

I use Thomas International to produce my DISC profiling reports (**www.thomasinternational.net**). Although there's plenty of other tools out there – including some free ones – I've found Thomas International reliable and their support and training incredibly good. They also insist you go through training and become accredited in feeding back results in a neutral, non-judgemental – and conversational – manner, which leads to better understanding. In my experience, free sites tend to provide 'canned' feedback which can lead to pigeonholing people.

As a High Dominance, High Influence person, I suspect I enjoy profiling because it helps me get the best out of people, motivate them and get the job done. If you want to get the best out of people, I really do encourage you to learn more about it.

If nothing else, it will help you appreciate and respect that we all have different strengths, and to take time to understand the type of task you want to delegate and the type of individual you should delegate it to.

Introverts and extroverts

The world is divided into introverts and extroverts – some more extreme than others.

This has nothing to do with DISC traits, any of which can belong to either an introvert or an extrovert.

Extroverts verbalise their thought process and speak more with their body and gestures, are comfortable in busy, public places and find networking natural.

Introverts, on the other hand, tend to think internally, are quieter, and don't enjoy having to mingle and chat. That's not to say they can't network – an introverted High Influence individual, for example, is often excellent at it – it's just that generally they don't welcome or enjoy it.

It's good to be reminded of this, because when you ask clients a question you'll usually be met with either a verbalised thought process or a silence, and the latter might encourage you to move on to another question. But don't – even if this means having to wait several minutes! Remember introverts need time to think things through and to reach a conclusion – at which point they'll be happy to share it with you.

A few years ago I was on a Board of Directors that, every six months, would hold a strategic retreat to which three non-executives were invited, to challenge our thinking and offer an external viewpoint.

One of the three non-executives – I'll call him Joe – was an extrovert, while one of our board members – I'll call him Mike – was an introvert. During our meetings, Mike would generally sit very quietly, staring at the floor, hand on chin and looking as if he wanted to have nothing to do with the conversation. Joe would often get incredibly annoyed at this and accuse Mike of having a hidden agenda, or of not being interested and not contributing.

In reality, what Mike was doing was thinking. Something someone had said had triggered a thought and he was building on it in his head until he was ready to share his idea (which, by the way, was generally fantastic).

The next time one of your clients responds to a question with silence, study them. Do they look as if they're deep in thought? If so, then they probably are. (If, on the other hand, they're staring back at you as if they're waiting for the next question, then that's probably true, too!)

If someone is deep in thought, be patient. Interrupting them might disrupt their thinking and destroy the seed of an idea. The best thing to do is wait until they comment – whether that's to say that they can't think of anything or to tell you what they've come up with.

With an extrovert client you'll hear every part of their thinking – from self-criticism through to self-indulgence and every point in between – which makes it much easier to know what's going on.

A great exercise, if a client is struggling to come up with an answer, is to get them to switch 'types.' I don't mean telling an introvert to become more extroverted but, if they've been unable to come up with anything, get them to talk through the problem and their thinking out loud. I'm not sure why, but often this seems to activate a different area of their brain and they're suddenly able to come up with a solution.

Although it's not quite as easy, you can also do the same with an extrovert. Get them to close their eyes and think through the situation without verbalising it.

Establishing a genuine connection

In the section on listening and specifically Level 5 listening – Tunnel focus - I referred to the importance of body language and how, when we're truly connected with what we're talking about, our body and tone convey our feelings about it. That's why it's important to observe people's bodies as much as possible and to listen to the tone and speed of their voices.

Think about it for a moment. Dogs know exactly how you're feeling just by looking at you. And a horse knows how confident you are, not from your words, but from your body.

Research suggests that when we communicate, the words we use contribute just 7% toward total comprehension. The tone and the speed at which they're delivered contribute 38%, while facial expressions, hand gestures and general body language contribute the remaining 55%.

With that in mind, it's easy to understand why emails and letters can often be misconstrued. And why it's often better to pick up the phone or – better still – arrange a face-to-face meeting.

The limbic region – the part that interprets body language – is the oldest, most primitive part of our brains, dating from a time before verbal language evolved. And, although we're rarely aware of it, it's still busily giving away and interpreting our feelings through our body movements and facial expressions.

Many years ago I attended Tony Robbins' three-day course – 'Unleash the Power Within' (an amazing experience that I can't recommend highly enough). At one point, he had us form groups of three with people we didn't know. The first person had to recall a specific moment from their past and allow his or her body to convey what they were reliving. (I don't mean by acting it out, but simply by really connecting with their memory and changing their stance and facial position etc in response).

The second person then had to mirror their body language, copying their stance, the position of their head and arms, their facial expression – in fact, everything – while the third person checked this was accurate and made any necessary tweaks to ensure the second person's body language exactly matched that of the first.

Afterwards, amazingly, the second person was able to explain what the first person was feeling. And, even more amazingly, in many cases they could pinpoint their exact memory. (To illustrate just how mind-blowing this was, in my group examples were 'going through a divorce' and 'waiting in a queue to ride a rollercoaster').

The reason for this is that not only do our bodies portray our emotional state but that the reverse can also happen – our emotional state can be influenced by our body. (That's why we're told "chin up" when we're feeling down).

You've probably noticed that watching something that makes you laugh can change your emotional state. Pretending to be happy, smiling and looking cheerful can, too.

A simple way to connect with someone you're talking to is to mirror their body language. Doing this will accomplish three things:

1. It will help you understand their state of mind.

2. It will create rapport.

3. It will give you a better chance of shifting their state of mind.

Establishing rapport leads to more effective communication because the person you're talking to starts to relax and open up. But be careful – if they shift posture don't mirror it instantly, do it gradually so it doesn't look obvious. If it's too blatant they're likely to become offended by what you're doing.

Done correctly though, before long you'll be in a state of natural rapport. If you'd like to see this in action, the next time you're out look for a group of friends standing having a drink at the bar. Odds are their bodies will be in perfect sync: all with one elbow on the bar, all with one leg casually crossed over the other, and all raising their glasses at exactly the same time. It's fascinating to watch – just don't overdo it!

Once you've established a rapport with your client, you may find you're able to take control and, if they're feeling upset or depressed about something, to nudge their posture to a more positive one. You can test this by shifting your posture slightly and seeing if they mirror you. If they do, then over the next 10-15 minutes continue to make small moves that gradually change their posture. Sit up a little straighter, lean forward, and so on. This will help them to feel more positive.

Being able to shift your client to a more positive physical – and thus mental – position will lead to much better conversations around how to improve things. Being worried or depressed suppresses our ability to think creatively.

Most importantly, establishing rapport helps to build trust and openness. Both of which are vital if you're to get the most from a coaching session.

Barriers to action

It's important to capture the ideas and work with your client to turn these in to actions, this is the point at which you relinquish control. You can't guarantee your client will implement the actions no matter how excited they are about them now. There are many reasons for this. We've looked at the change journey and in addition, when somebody returns back to their business it's like landing back on a tread mill that's moving at 12 miles per hour.

In Part 3 we'll address prioritising and in addition here are a few techniques you can use to improve the chances of them setting aside some time to take the action that will inevitably lead to them having more time. (It might not be necessary to use these if your client is an action taker. Use your judgement).

Motivators: Pain and gain

We've looked at the change journey and the importance of the emotional as well as the logical impact, at the need to emphasise the pain of not doing something as well as the gain of doing it.

Sometimes, people have simply become used to how things are. Things could be better, but it would take effort. Helping them recognise the consequences of action will improve the chances of them taking it.

Deadlines

It's amazing how much impetus can materialise when a deadline is looming. Something in our heads kicks in and makes stuff – stuff we've been putting off and putting off – happen. But missing a deadline needs to have consequences if we're to take it seriously. If not, it's just another date in the diary.

When you're working out deadlines with clients, agree on some consequences – you can make this discussion fun, but don't forget its serious intent.

Would you break a promise?

Often I simply ask my client "Would you break a promise?" Invariably their answer will be "No." I then ask if they're prepared to promise that they'll complete what I identify as the most important action on their list.

What might stop you?

Once you've identified this action, talk them through it and through the next few days/weeks/months. Is anything coming up that might stop them completing it? After this, ask them to imagine it's the next session and they're telling you they weren't able to do it. What reason might they give?

This encourages clients to consider everything that could possibly get in their way. It also helps prevent them using this as an excuse at the next session!

I can't do this until...

Fear of action disguises itself in many ways. One is rationalising why something can't happen yet: "I'll stop smoking when I'm less stressed." "I'll focus on this when that happens." Sometimes there may be a genuine reason, but for the most part it's simply worry and the brain working overtime to come up with excuses. Explore these. Ask why the reasons should prevent action being taken.

Help them delegate actions

"Only do what only you can do." I took this learning from Stephen Covey's book 'The 7 habits of Highly Effective People'.

As the owner of a business it's important to act as the conductor of the orchestra rather than as one of the musicians – and certainly rather than trying to be both!

Unfortunately, delegating isn't as easy as simply asking someone to do a job. It sounds like it should be, but often what we get back isn't what we expected, or the job doesn't get done at all.

Delegation, done properly, should help people to grow. It should help them to feel valued and understand the importance of what they do. Although it can take time to become really effective at delegation, the rewards are huge. Not only will the job be done to the standard you require, you'll also be free to focus on the more important aspects of your role.

People often say "But by the time I've explained how to do something, I might as well do it myself." If the task really is a one-off that can be done quickly then perhaps that's true. But how many genuinely one-off jobs are there?

If it's a job that comes up often then it's worth investing time in training someone to free up your time in the future. Even if it's a genuinely one-off project, but one that will require considerable time to undertake, it should be delegated.

Start by identifying items on your client's 'to-do' list that can be delegated. In Part 3 I describe the use of the four quadrants under the heading 'Prioritising' (page 82). Use this to identify what your client really shouldn't be doing and start with these.

Challenge them on why someone else can't do them – many people simply find it difficult to let go or to accept that others can do certain tasks.

Once you've agreed which tasks can be delegated, for the process to be effective you now need to tease all the relevant information from your client's head. Without this, it's easy to omit important details which will lead to questions further down the line, or to the job being done badly.

I've provided a structured process that you can go through with your client and that they can use when delegating. This can be found in the appendix at the back of this book. Refer to Appendix 3 – Effective delegation for the detailed process.

Nagging rights

This description may sound a little off-putting and unfortunately nagging is often something that men associate with their wife. However, it works!

People, not just men, need to be nagged. There's an expression, 'he who shouts loudest.' People need to be reminded of what's important to them, especially when they return to their daily grind and are back in their typical working environment attending to demands on their time.

Asking "Can I hold you to that? Do you mind if I follow this up in a week's time to see how you've got on?" is simple and yet very powerful.

The psychological impact of knowing that you have to face the person to whom you've made a commitment and tell them you haven't done it is huge. It makes the chances of action being taken that much higher.

That's why you should put in your diary to call, visit or even text every certain amount of days to follow their progress.

Be the support

If action still isn't taken, work with your client to overcome whatever's preventing them. Explore what got in the way and what's holding them back. Although holding someone accountable is good, don't be too harsh. It might prevent them attending their next session or taking your next call.

Part 3
Small Gains,
Big Difference

Marginal gains

A business is simply a means to an end. It's there to work for its owner and to give them the life they want. Any change – increasing profits, implementing efficiencies – should lead to freeing up their time so they can spend it doing things they enjoy outside work or, inside work, as an entrepreneurial business owner rather than as an employee always running to stay still.

Marginal gains, as a concept, means to break something down to its constituent parts and then to make small enhancements to each. Individually these tweaks may only have a very small impact, but together, their synergy can be significant.

In this section we're not going to look at a six-step process to quadruple sales overnight as you might find advertised on the internet. Instead, we're going to focus on different aspects of running a business and making relatively small changes to each.

Sometimes, of course, a client may have so many fires to fight that conversation will have to centre on the challenges at hand. However, although they do need to address these, unless they make causal changes, they'll always be running around chasing their tail. To avoid this, they need to spend time working on – not in – their business.

Now let's take a look at the ways you can help clients improve how they manage their time and effectiveness.

What are the numbers that matter?

It's important to understand someone's dreams and aspirations for what they intend their business to achieve for them personally. Not everyone is ready to share their dreams and aspirations to start with. As a starting point and as an accountant, it's better to ease your client into talking about their dreams by focusing on what they expect of you, the numbers.

Something that's incredibly effective at starting a conversation, at opening people up to new possibilities, is to find out and understand the numbers that really matter to them. What they are now and what they'd like them to be.

A good way to do this, towards the end of an accounts meeting with a client, is to grab a sheet of paper and a pen. Create three columns on the right-hand side of the page, leaving a larger column on the left. Head up the columns on the right 'Now,' '5 years' and 'Gap.' In the left column write 'Sales,' beneath this 'Profit,' and then, in the 'Now' column, write down their current sales and profit figures.

You're then ready to say something along the following lines:

"John, just looking at your current sales and profit figures, can I ask you a question? If you could wave a magic wand, what would those figures look like five years from now?"

Once you've got their response, seek to understand the emotional impact of those figures by asking, "Why is that important to you?" or "How will you personally benefit from that?"

Next, ask what other numbers are important to them. The hours they work? The number of out-of-hours phone calls they receive? The number of holidays they can take per year? How often those holidays are interrupted? How much people rely on them?

For each answer, look at what they'd like those numbers to be in five years' time, then find out where they are now. If they say "I'll probably still be working those hours in five years' time" remind them about the magic wand. Ask them to consider what their ideal life would look like, rather than one based on their current circumstances.

Again, seek to understand the emotional impact "Why is that important to you?" "How would you personally benefit?" "What would it feel like?" "If you were to achieve those numbers how would you celebrate?" "How would you feel if you didn't achieve those numbers?"

By the end of the session you might end up with something that looks like this:

	Now	5 Years	Gap
Sales	£246,000	£750,000	£504,000
Profits	£77,000	£250,000	£173,000
Take home	£50,000	£150,000	£100,000
Business Value	£246,000	£750,000	£504,000
Personal Wealth	£200,000	£700,000	£500,000
Hours per week	60 – 80	35	c 35
Holidays per year	1 week	10 weeks	9 weeks
Reliance in business	100%	20%	80%

Not only does completing this allow you to ascertain the numbers that matter to them, it also gives you a gap to work to. So, ask the questions "What if I could help you close those gaps? What would that be worth to you? What if in five years' time those numbers were a reality?"

Although they'll probably respond in a pessimistic tone, go on to say "Let me demonstrate how we might close this gap..." Point to the profit gap and explain about the six sales growth drivers (described shortly in this book), exploring the idea that best fits their business. See what additional ideas come up, and then calculate the potential impact these may have. Keep the numbers sensible. Simply work out 1% or 2% increases to the sales figure and accommodate any impact on overheads or cost of sales. Give them an idea of what their profit figure could look like with just that small improvement and then extrapolate this over a five-year period.

Even if you don't get close to their ideal number, you've demonstrated how – in just a few short minutes – you've narrowed the gap considerably.

This process is great to use as part of the promoting your business growth services as explained in Part 4.

Discover their dream

Why is your client in business? What are their aspirations and goals? What do they hope their business will look like in five years' time? Or their personal situation? How will the business help them achieve this?

These are important – 'big picture' – questions.

The reasons people set up a business are unique to each of them. Some did so to make things better in the world, while others simply didn't want to work for someone else. Sometimes it's down to nothing more than progression within a long-established business.

It's important to bring your client back to their particular "why." The day-to-day running of a business can be so hectic that they forget the bigger picture. Everyone's strategic thinking is limited when they're too busy juggling to have time to stop and think.

Start by seeking to understand their personal goals so you can help them shape their business to better reflect this. Asking them why they set up their business is a good place to start. Perhaps they wanted more freedom, to escape a 9-5 regime, working five days per week with limited holidays? (If so, chances are they're now working harder, longer and with even less time off).

If that's the case, then find out why freedom's important to them. What did they want to do with it? Explore the world? Spend more time with their children? Focus on understanding the bigger picture so you can help them achieve their goals.

Once a business owner believes this is 'just how it is' they no longer see the bigger picture. They've filed their dreams away in the 'not possible' folder. Before you can help them to turn their dreams into reality though, they'll need to rediscover them. So here are a couple of questions to get them started:

- If you could wave a magic wand...

- If anything were possible...

- If someone gave you three wishes, what would they be?

- What was your defining moment? What was it that triggered your need to establish your business? What did you hope to achieve back then?

Their answers can be as out there as they want. The important thing is to re-open that door. It's unlikely their answer will be "A two-week cruise around the Caribbean, and then back to normal please." They're more likely to describe their ideal lifestyle or how they've changed the world in some way.

Make sure you understand what's important about each desire. Always ask "Why is that so important to you?" Keep drilling down. Only then will you understand what's really important to them. And don't be surprised if a client makes a sudden U-turn by saying "Actually, that's not what I'd wish for at all. Here's what's really important to me..." Because you've re-opened the door to all the possibilities out there, they're simply remembering what really matters.

Write down your client's aspirations. If you've asked "When would you like that to happen?" and they've answered "Now!" ask them what's stopping them.

A client of mine was asked this very question. One of his three wishes was to drop everything and go to Uganda to provide aid. When asked "What's stopping you doing that right now?" he thought for a few moments and then said "Nothing."

Within a couple of month's he'd put his affairs in order and done exactly that. The only thing that had been stopping him was that he'd been so busy for so long that he'd forgotten what he was being busy for. He just needed time out to think about what really mattered. We often put so many things on our wish lists that we forget to come back and check whether now would be a good time to do them.

So, find out what's stopping your client from achieving their goals. Often the answer will be business related: "I just don't get the time out of the business that I'd like to." "It's not generating the income I need." "I'd need to sell the business for X and it's not worth anything like that right now." Once you've done this, you can help your client paint a picture of what their business might need to look like if they're to achieve those goals.

And remember: never make assumptions. It might not be about giving the owner more free time. If they set up their business to change the world in some way, then working less hours or earning more income may not be important. What's important is moving closer to their purpose.

Once you're sure your picture of their personal and business aspirations is correct, and you understand how their business will need to look to achieve it, you have your client's vision. Now document this with them and encourage them to share it with everyone they work with, from customers through to employees, partners and even suppliers.

Initially, their vision might appear to be locked on the far side of a glass ceiling. That's why it's important to construct a ladder which, just like the ladders you use at home, will have rungs to take them to where they want to go – and one step at a time, the journey seems less daunting. (Can you imagine how hard life would be without a loft ladder? First you'd need to shift some furniture around to stand on, then you'd have to balance precariously before using the last of your strength to haul yourself up the final few feet).

Construct the ladder using clear goals and milestones, each with its own timeline. And set specific dates, rather than "in five years' time," because it's all too easy for that to keep slipping. Draw a line in the sand and agree to it. (Of course it doesn't have to be five years, it could be twenty – or two).

Help your client identify both the big and the little steps they'll need to take by brainstorming (in the way I described in Part 2). Get them to think of as many things as possible that might need to happen if they're to achieve their vision.

Once you've done this, work with your client to group the steps into progressive milestones and determine what the business will look like at each one. What will the important numbers be? The important numbers can be turnover, margins, profits. They could be vision related – people affected/impacted (depending on the vision of course) or personal, hours working, holidays taken. Most likely a combination.

Start with the end in mind and then map out their journey – the steps they need to take to get there. Sometimes it might be easier to work back from the end, while for others it'll be easier to go forward.

When, in 1961, John F Kennedy announced that NASA would put a man on the moon before the end of the decade, NASA asked him to retract the target, stating it simply wasn't possible. When he refused, they had to work out what to do. In the end, they worked backwards. They envisioned the final outcome and simply asked "What happened just before that?" made a note and then repeated the process until they'd got a complete set of steps to follow.

Keep asking the question "If, in five years' time, you've achieved this vision, what happened just before that?"

Aim high and think positive

As I mentioned previously, accountants by nature can often be cautious and avoid risk, but most of the best businesses out there and the technology we enjoy in our lives are born of our risk and determination to pursue a dream despite the odds. It's a difficult stance to take but don't douse out the fire, remain neutral in building the idea especially at the LEARNING stage. If you have worries about certain aspects by all means raise these during the SOLVING stage, but let the idea get some legs.

Whether or not you believe your client's vision to be practical – and realistic within the timelines set – keep helping them explore that vision rather than voice concern.

You'll often find that it's the big audacious goals – rather than the realistic ones – that really focus people's minds. Our minds love a challenge and sometimes a really big challenge has a funny way of making our brains move up a gear.

We need to think big and aim high so please, never put doubt in clients' minds. In fact, why not try to get them to think bigger? Ask them what they might do if the deadline were half the current period, if the goal were twice as big, or the competition an even greater threat. Make the challenge bigger.

Working with the right clients

"It is more important to acquire customers who count than it is to count the customers you acquire" - Tom Connellan, New York Times best-selling author and popular keynote speaker

A common mistake I come across with businesses (accountants included) is that they will cast a wide net in their marketing activity. They'll take on any customer if they feel they can deliver. Sounds logical; customers = income. It does, but that income tends to be competitive income.

Trying to be all things to all people prevents your ability to call yourself an expert in one field, it prevents you from differentiating yourself from the competition. If others in your industry are offering the same products and services as you are, all prospective customers can do to ensure they're getting the best deal is to compare prices and negotiate using the competition as leverage. As a consequence it prevents you from charging a premium, instead you have to charge competitively.

Rather than casting a wide net, encourage your client to consider their main area of expertise and what they enjoy doing the most. Develop a list of criterion that describes the type of customer they prefer to work with from a personality point of view. What are the types of jobs they prefer to do? Conversely, what do they not enjoy doing?

Then, help your client come up with an ideal customer profile and encourage them to focus on just that type of work with those types of customers. To use the descriptions in their marketing, to add much more value around delivering on those services and position themselves as specialists in those specific areas. People will naturally pay more for a specialist than a generalist.

To summarise the big picture session, I'll end this section with some do's:

- Make sure every goal you set with your client is concise and is worded in such a way that there's no room for misinterpretation.

- If possible, word it in the past tense. Doing so describes the finished goal in a way that means you (your client) did it.

- Set clear deadlines and markers – using numbers where possible to ensure your client knows when they've got there.

- Help your client create a clear statement of why their goal is so important.

- Be sure to map all the actions back to the present moment. Which single action can they take today to set the ball rolling? Whilst their enthusiasm is high, encourage them to take that first step. It may help them truly commit to the actions they've agreed.

And some don'ts:

- Avoid creating goals around increasing revenue. As an accountant you should know that increasing revenue is meaningless if the profits are poor. But, because accountancy practices are still sold based on gross recurring revenues, many of the accountants I've worked with continue to focus on it.

- That said, don't just focus on increasing profits either. Profits are a consequence of great work. Focus on this, on how your client can achieve it. What do they want to be remembered for? Whatever it is, it's sure to be unique to them, which means it'll also be the added value they can build into their fee structure to generate the profits from.

Prioritising

Most business owners are desperately juggling lots of balls. Sometimes, some of these can be ditched, or shelved for a later date, but when they're all in the air it can be difficult to make that call – they all seem really important. Luckily, there are several techniques to help them improve how they prioritise work.

One of the ones I use is from Stephen Covey's book '7 Habits of Highly Effective People'. It looks like this:

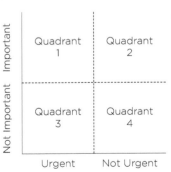

Quadrant 1: Urgent and important. Like a fire, it needs to be fought first, but it's also important to identify the root cause to prevent it happening again.

Quadrant 2: Important, but not urgent. Things that need to be done if the business is to improve – but things from Q1 and Q3 keep getting in the way.

Quadrant 3: Urgent, but not that important. Could they be delegated? Or a decision made as to whether they really need doing? It might be just that someone's shouting loudly for it.

Quadrant 4: Not urgent or important. Things that need to be eliminated.

Give your client a pack of Post-it notes and ask them to write down everything they can think of that they should be working on. One item per Post-it and in no particular order. Then ask them to add everything from their diary, in-tray and inbox.

Once they've done this, I put a static flipchart-sized dry wipe sheet on the wall, make up the grid and ascertain which quadrant each item falls into. You may have to challenge each and every Post-it, though, and it's not always easy. How about something that's urgent and important but which could be delegated, for example? In this case, I'd suggest you make it a Q3 leaving Q1 for the things your client has to do personally.

I then use another matrix to work out which of the Q1 and Q2 items need to be done first – it's a great way of checking that they really do need doing.

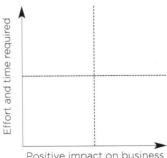

Note that the arrangement of numbers in the boxes have changed. If an item is low effort and high impact then it's a quick win, so they should do it first. How about high effort, low impact though? In that case, ask if it's worth doing at all. It may well be, but never simply accept this without exploring and challenging it. Sometimes something might not have an immediate impact, but its long-term impact would be really high. If so, move it to the high impact box.

To end the session, you should assign each Post-it note a specific date to be done by, and help to break down any that turn out to be projects into concrete actions.

Getting – and getting more from – customers

Increasing revenue can be broken down into seven sales growth drivers:

1. Pricing for maximum profit.

2. Getting more leads.

3. Converting leads into customers.

4. Getting customers to buy more.

5. Getting customers to buy more often.

6. Getting customers to stay longer.

7. Consistency and Automation.

Making just small tweaks to each of these can have a huge impact. Use your skills with numbers to show the potential impact on your client's business, quantifying the benefits of their implementation – or of tailored variations of them which arise from your conversations.

('How to Build a Better Business and Make More Money' by Mark Wickersham and Steve Pipe is a great book which covers these drivers in more detail. I recommend you use it to complement your Business Advisory Services. You can also check out this website for further guidance: **www.improveyourpractice.co.uk**).

Through AVN, accountants can access the world's only marginal gains profit improvement software, called 'Simple Stuff That Works', which uses this exact framework to help you take your client systematically and easily through the process of improving profitability.

It's important to remember that these ideas apply to your practice as well as for you to share and explore with your clients. On this basis when you read the following, apply it to your practice first.

1. Pricing for maximum profit

Everybody wants more sales but, although these might bump up revenue, they can also make the business owner much busier, meaning – unless the owner is pricing profitably – he simply becomes a busy fool. However, very few people understand how to price appropriately. Most simply look at their competitors and strive to undercut them. If they don't have any like-for-like competitors, then they'll look for something similar or assign a value to their time and charge by the hour.

Charging by the hour is one of the worst ways to charge. People often assume you'll simply take longer in order to be able to charge more. In theory, it also means that the more experienced you become, the more efficiently you can do a piece of work, the less you'll earn. It simply undervalues your experience and knowledge.

If you ask clients whether increasing or decreasing their prices would improve business, they'd probably suggest decreasing them – or even offering a discount to tempt new customers. Although this is a strategy employed by many, it can frustrate customers who will challenge the fee when it goes back up, or move elsewhere. This is what happens when price is the deciding factor.

I'm now going to put forward two scenarios and, as a practicing accountant, I'd like you to consider your own response to them. (Although you can use exactly the same script with your clients, so be sure to remember it).

Firstly, imagine a small accountancy practice that's still getting established. It has an annual revenue of £200,000 and overheads – offices and a small team – of £140,000. In order to reflect a true profit, let's say the accountant takes a salary of £40,000, which leaves a profit of £20,000.

If you decreased your fees by 10%, you'd reduce profit by £20,000 – leaving yourself out of pocket. But, you'll probably argue at this point, decreasing your fees would attract more clients. Well, I'm afraid to report that you'd have to get 11.11% more clients simply to break even, to generate the same profit you were generating before. In short, you'd be earning less per client and working harder for the same amount.

Now let's flip that.

If you put your prices up by 1% or 2%, do you think you'd lose any clients? Unlikely, isn't it? If the price of beer went up by that amount there wouldn't be a mass exodus from the bar. One or two people might have a bit of a grumble, but they'd get over it pretty quickly.

What if you put your prices up by 5% or 10%? What percentage of customers do you think you might lose then? And which clients would be most likely to leave? Your best clients? Or the ones which give you the most grief? In fact, you could lose over 9% of your clients before your profit would be worse. In short, you'd be earning the same but working less.

Remember, increasing your prices is always the better option.

I'd like to share a pertinent story with you. Firstly, by way of setting the scene, AVN is the name of my business. It's an association of accountants who subscribe for membership to AVN. We help them implement the changes we advocate in their practice that make their accountancy business run more profitably and more enjoyably. In addition we help them add much more value around the accounts and deliver business advisory services to their clients.

Let me tell you about Simon, who's an accountant and one of our clients at AVN. His circumstances when he first became a client were that he was working incredibly long hours, serving lots of clients, and not really earning the income he should have been. We went through this process with him and encouraged him to increase his prices. It took him quite some time to pluck up the courage, but eventually he wrote to all his clients informing them that his fee was increasing by 10%. He then sat back and braced himself for the phone to ring with complaints. But – nothing. No one left. In fact, no one batted an eyelid.

As part of this process, Simon had also gone through all of his clients and graded them A - D. A were the great clients – profitable, nice and he enjoyed the type of work he did for them. D, however, were the opposite – unprofitable, and not particularly nice to work with. Although he'd decided he was happy to lose the D clients, in the end he didn't lose any clients at all, which meant he was earning more, but still working really hard – and sometimes for not very nice people.

So, he decided to increase his fees further. He sent another letter stating that they'd go up by another 10% and braced himself for the complaints. But again, nothing. No loss of clients – not even a complaint. Which meant his income was much better again, but he was still working long hours.

It was only when he put his prices up for a third time that he started to meet price resistance – and even then, only from a few people he'd already identified as D clients (and not all of them, either).

For Simon, the process was pivotal in turning his practice around, and he went on to transform it into a profitable, scalable business that could flourish without him needing to be involved in the day-to-day operational aspects. (In fact, he went on to create another business).

Helping your clients improve their pricing will allow them to generate more income while working fewer hours.

Helping accountants earn better fees

Many businesses – accountancy practices are no exception – don't sell their services very well. They certainly don't sell the value of what they do. By focusing on the features of what they provide instead of the benefits those features bring, they fail to add value to their services. And, when it comes to pricing, this leaves them only one option: to undercut the competition.

Although many people assume that everyone wants the cheapest option, it's not true. In fact, only a minority do. Most of us are happy to pay for good service and value as long as we believe the value outweighs the cost.

When AVN begins to work with an accountant, we nearly always meet resistance around pricing. They assume that no one will buy their services if someone down the road is cheaper. However, their services are only sought after because they're a legal requirement – they're not something that are valued in themselves. By helping our accountants add value to their clients, they're able to increase their average fee several times over (in some cases by up to ten times). And this doesn't mean they're ripping clients off – if anything, the opposite.

AVN accountants earn higher fees, work fewer hours and – because much of the value they deliver is in helping their clients grow – have a much higher sense of purpose than in previous years.

As long as what you offer is sufficiently different from the competition, price no longer becomes the comparison.

In a simple exercise that will most likely add a few thousand pounds to your – and your clients' – bottom line, I recommend you put your prices up by a minimum of 1%.

Go for it!

---

2. Getting more leads

Many businesses create a website then sit back and wait for the phone to ring. A website, however, is simply an online brochure: it should explain what the business does, its benefits, and then give clear steps on how to find out more. (Preferably via a 'capture page' which collects the visitor's email address).

Websites are so plentiful that expecting yours to be found through a search engine is optimistic at best. My strategy for getting more leads is therefore around getting great referrals from your existing clients.

Do you remember the mistake I mentioned – in the earlier section on open/closed questions – that many people make when asking for referrals? How they'll ask "Do you know anyone else we could work with?"

Instead of falling into this same trap, start by mapping out your ideal client profile: the type of industry they work in, perhaps how big their company is, what sort of person they are. If they work with consumers, describe what their customers would be like or, if they work on houses, what sort of houses. You need to build a clear and concise description of the type of client you want to work with. The better the description, the more likely it is that someone will be able to think of someone exactly like that. (I often see on accountants' websites that they're happy to work with any industry, and businesses of any size. It's too general. It makes it too difficult for someone to home in on who they know that you might want to work with).

Once your profile's complete, but before you ask your current clients who they know like that, remember to:

1. Consider the timing.

2. Give an accurate description about the type of referral needed (to help focus their minds).

3. Never just ask for one name.

Also, before you ask a client for a referral, always make sure they're happy with your work. In fact, try to ensure they're elated with it. Simply ask how happy they are on a scale of 1 to 10 (where 10 is elated and 1 is extremely disappointed). If they give less than 7, you need to understand why and to put it right. If they give more than 7, however, then use the following script:

"I'm really pleased to have done a great job for you. In fact, as it's people like you I enjoy working with most, I wonder if you could help me. As I'm looking to work with more great customers, can I share with you my ideal customer profile so you can tell me who you know who fits that profile? I'm looking for three names."

What you're doing here is both flattering them, and painting a picture of the type of person you're looking for. By asking for three names you're making their brain work a little harder. If you asked for one, you'd get between 0 and 1. If you ask for three, you'll get between 0 and 3 – which improves your chances.

Once they've come up with some names, write each one down. Then go back and ask for a little more information about each. Choose the one that appeals most, and ask your client if they'd be kind enough to introduce you – either in person or by email. A personal introduction will greatly improve your chances of setting up a meeting.

Although there are many strategies you can use to increase leads, I find asking for referrals brings the warmest ones. And best of all, it's free.

3. Converting leads into customers

Although some people worry that this will be the most difficult step, it's a myth that you need to have a certain personality to be good at selling. It's true – if you think back to my Understanding People section – that a High Influence person is probably naturally good at it. But it's also true that a 'hard sell' approach often leads to buyer remorse, when customers begin to regret their decision.

You need to ensure that neither you nor the clients you're trying to help feel afraid of selling, and that – rather than experience remorse – those you sell to feel great about their purchase.

As long as it's set out correctly, a brochure is a great way to do this.

Remember, you shouldn't simply give a brochure to a prospective customer and then expect them to come back later to buy something. It should act as a guide when delivering a sales pitch.

Creating a brochure forces you to really think things through. What problem is your product trying to fix? How does it provide a solution? What are its features and benefits?

All great sales people use predetermined scripts. They work through a specific structure, starting with the problem the prospect is likely to have, and then working through to the sale. It's rehearsed. It's polished. It's extremely well thought through and, of course, it's tweaked regularly.

A brochure not only acts as an aide-mémoire for the person selling, it looks impressive too. If a prospective customer needs time to reflect before making their decision they can take it away to read later. If they decide to buy, they can take it away to remind themselves of the benefits of their purchase – which means they're less likely to experience buyer remorse. (Or they can even use it to explain to others why they've made the purchase).

Remember to tell a story. Word your brochure as though you're speaking directly to someone and demonstrate that you understand their problem.

Below is my nine-step process to creating a high-quality brochure. (Of course, if what you're selling sits on a shelf in a shop, a brochure may not be appropriate).

i. Describe the pain/problem/challenge
What are the problems your product can fix? Why are they problems? Be specific. Describe three different problems if need be, rather than using broad brushstrokes.

ii. Describe the big-picture benefits of removing that pain
Don't go into detail yet. Simply describe what life might be like without the problem. Would things happen faster? Be less stressful? Or might they finally have their finger on the pulse?

iii. How your product or service can take them from pain to gain
Take them through the journey. Keep it brief but describe how your product or service can overcome their problem. Will it be a painless journey? Will they receive support along the way?

iv. Describe the hierarchical packages you offer
If possible, break your product down into three options or service levels. A top – all singing all dancing – level packed with bundled-in extras, followed by a middle and a low level, the latter offering perhaps the bare minimum. (People like choice, but three options are enough. Consider Starbucks' three sizes of coffee, or Apple's three versions of its iPhone, each with different memory capacity).

Even purchasing a fridge can offer a top level which includes delivery, fitting, and taking your old fridge away; a middle one of delivery only; and a basic, purchase-only option. Although it's the same product, you're accommodating different needs. Describe each level. Don't go into detail at this point, stick to the big-picture benefits and give each level a title such as 'gold,' 'silver,' and 'bronze,' (You'll find most people will go for the middle option). For example, you could say:

"Our gold-level service means you won't need to do anything. We'll arrange delivery on a day that's convenient for you, and then collect your old fridge at the same time."

v. Break the elements down and allocate them to packages
Create a grid that lists all the features on the left-hand side. List everything that's included in the high-level option. Then, on the right-hand side, create three columns, one for each of the three service levels you've created and title them

appropriately, for example 'gold,' 'silver' and 'bronze.'
Finally, put a tick or a cross in each box depending on
whether the feature is included. (There's a reason you'll have
seen so many of these grids on websites – they work).

vi. What it all means

Remember that features mean little to customers. Features
are only really appreciated by the seller, who needs to
translate them into benefits and into what they actually mean
for customers. You could even title this section 'What it all
means...' Then list each feature and describe its benefits – in
emotional terms, if possible. To return to our fridge analogy,
you might write:

*Installation: "Don't run the risk of scratching your new fridge –
or your floor. Our experienced installers and their specialist
equipment make manoeuvring your fridge easy, and they'll also
ensure it's up and running before they leave. In the unlikely event
that anything does go wrong, they're also fully insured so you can
rest assured it'll be taken care of."*

Do this for each feature.

vii. Bolt-ons and their benefits

Are there any options that aren't included even in your gold
service? If you've ever used Apple's website you'll have
noticed that each of their products is broken down into three
options. But, as soon as you've chosen one, you're
immediately offered further bolt-ons.

Remember this brochure will be used by the person selling the
product or service. By this point, the discussion over service
levels has already taken place and the customer has selected
their product. As this means they're now in buying mode, it's the
perfect opportunity to showcase your bolt-ons or compatible
products.

viii. Case studies and testimonials

People need evidence that your product or service works, and
the best evidence is case studies from satisfied customers.

Case studies should be in the form of a story, one that starts with how difficult things were before your product came to their rescue, and then moves on to how things are now. (A useful tip is to follow steps one, three and two – in that order – of this brochure creation formula). If possible, give each case study a punchy headline, preferably using a comment from within it.

A testimonial can be much shorter, and is more likely to be simply advocating the product. Short testimonials can be scattered throughout your brochure in the form of quotes from customers.

ix. Closing thoughts – Why you/your business strives for a better world
Leave customers understanding your "why." Why you believe in your product or why you want to make the world a better place. Also, why should they pick you? What are you reputed for specifically?

Once you've completed all nine steps, send the document to your graphic designer with photos of the people who've given case studies and testimonials (it helps to reinforce that they're genuine). It may also be worth separating out some one-liners to distribute as quotes throughout the brochure.

That nine step system is one I've successfully used to create brochures for my business and to create brochures for AVN's clients to use within their accountancy practice to promote their products and services. Of course they're able to tailor the brochure to fit with their own style.

At the end of the selling process, it's important to check that the prospective customer is happy to go ahead. If they say "yes," what forms do they need to complete and how do they pay? Ensure the process is clear.

If the prospective customer says "no," however, your team should seek to understand why. Gently find out what's holding them back. Most likely, they just need more information.

An effective high-quality brochure can really improve how you package your product or service, significantly increasing its perceived value and making you stand out from the competition.

4. Getting customers to buy more

In the previous section I referred to how bolt-ons and upselling are a great way to get customers to buy more without resorting to a hard-sell approach. In many cases, you'll be doing them a favour by letting them know about additional products and services you offer.

Similarly, customers often may not know about other ways you can help them.

That's why I'd now like to share some great questions with you that will lead to your customers purchasing more.

Consider what happens when you visit a McDonalds. You look at the menu, see the big juicy burger, go to the counter and ask for it. The sales assistant immediately asks, "Would you like fries with that?" You'll most likely agree. Their next question is "Would you like to upgrade to a meal and get a drink too?" Again you nod. You've just been upsold to. Your spend increased by more than an extra 80%.

If you started by asking for a meal, they'll have asked if you wanted to go large. There's always a question you can use to upsell – but the assistant doesn't feel like they're selling, and the consumer doesn't feel they're being sold to. They simply reply "Yes, please" or "No, thank you."

Another example. Imagine you're a shop owner. A man walks in, buys a torch and leaves – only to return a half hour later looking annoyed because he didn't get batteries with it. How many other instances can you think of where one product complements another? If you have a repertoire of questions such as "Would you like some batteries with that?" not only are you getting your customers to buy more, you're also doing them a favour by pointing out things they might need.

Make sure you work with your client to come up with some great questions that help them bolt on additional products.

5. Getting customers to buy more often

My wallet is full of loyalty cards. Whether it's saving stick-on cups of coffee from McDonald's or collecting stamps of a certain brand of beer, people like to think they're getting something for free. Loyalty cards are a great way to do this – and to make sure they buy from you more often.

You don't have to present a loyalty card in a physical format either. You could just as easily offer a ratcheting discount scheme for frequent purchasing. And you don't have to stop at loyalty cards – there are many other simple strategies you can use, too.

Let's imagine, for example, that Jane gets her hair coloured roughly every couple of months, and although her hairdresser relies on Jane coming in, she can never guarantee the exact date. Now imagine that Jane's left booking her appointment – and this time it's for a special occasion, a holiday, or a wedding – to the last minute and her hairdresser is fully booked? The odds are Jane will go elsewhere. She may even come away happier and change her hairdresser.

What if, instead of this scenario, after each appointment Jane's hairdresser asks, "Jane, are you happy with your hair?" When she replies that she is, her hairdresser can suggest they put an appointment in the diary for six weeks' time. The likelihood is Jane will agree and the appointment is booked. Not only does this work for Jane – she doesn't have to rely on noticing her roots are showing before she books her next appointment, when she might have to wait a while – it works for her hairdresser too – she has a definite date in her diary and for sooner than normal.

If her hairdresser makes this question part of her system, she'll increase the average number of times Jane comes in each year from six to eight. That's a 33% increase. By extending this same service to every customer, she'd increase her revenue and improve customer retention.

6. Getting customers to stay longer

Although it's easier to retain customers than to convert new ones, many businesses fail to focus on this as much as they could. Instead of fixing their leaking bucket around customer retention, they exert effort in marketing and selling to new ones.

There are three questions for you or your client to consider here:

1. Are your customers getting what they expect when they expect it?

2. Are they dazzled by your customer service at every point of contact?

3. Do you handle complaints well?

People tend to move on when their expectations aren't met, when they're not treated well or listened to. Performing regular – at least annual – customer feedback surveys will help you answer all three questions and allow you to put right any wrongs.

Other tips include ensuring new customers have a document detailing exactly what is and what isn't included in the level of service they've selected.

Regularly brainstorm ways that customers can be wowed every time they interact with you or your team. But remember: if you wow a customer today they will expect it as part of the normal service going forward. Maintain your standards and keep raising the bar.

7. Consistency and automation

Following a process allows you to achieve the same consistent result each time. If you leave things to chance, or to memory, you can never predict the result.

This section is around ensuring that the methods I've mentioned, and the ideas that are developed during conversations with your clients, are tried and tested and become the norm across their business. In other words, they become a system that must be followed by everyone in the company.

Remember the example I gave of the standard McDonald's question "Would you like fries with that?" This isn't just training, it's a system. Whether prompts pop up on the assistants' tills, or they have the questions set out in front of them, a system exists to remind them of their training. No matter how long the queue of people waiting to be served, each customer will be asked the same questions.

Systems are an essential part of any business because they lead to consistency. They certainly don't prevent innovation as some might assume. In fact, if someone has an idea for improving the system, then there should equally be a system for capturing, testing, implementing and making the new idea part of the existing system.

Systems aren't simply used for franchise reasons. They're used because they help business owners improve the delegation of roles, which in the past, they'd have often had to play themselves. I'll be returning to the topic of systems in the section entitled 'Help them get their life back' on page 100.

If you'd like to learn more about the seven drivers, and add even more great ideas to your repertoire, go to:
www.improveyourpractice.co.uk

Improving productivity

This is a subject I'm passionate about. Particularly as, despite all the technology that's around today which is meant to be making us much more productive, the reverse is often the case.

I believe that for most of the day many of us are only about 10% as productive as we could be. For those of you who are not convinced, let me explain a little further.

Now, imagine you're driving along a straight road for 100 miles.

As your car is a manual and there are traffic lights every few hundred yards, no sooner do you shift up a gear than you have to stop at a red light and go back down to first, before beginning the acceleration routine all over again. If this were the case, it would take you a very long time to go that 100 miles, wouldn't it? In fact, you'd never really get out of first gear. The ideal, of course, would be that you'd go up through all the gears, reach the highest, and then cruise along at high speed without having to stop again.

Well, our brains work in a similar fashion. They also have to go through the equivalent of a set of gears in order to reach their maximum level of concentration. It takes around 11 minutes for this to happen, but any interruption will take our brains back to the beginning, just like the car hitting a set of traffic lights.

What makes matters worse is that at least in a car we can see what gear we're in and the speed we're going at. It's clear when our progress isn't perfect. But, where our brains are concerned, after an interruption most of us think we simply switch back to our work and return to full speed. Studies show, however, that it's not the case.

Any interruption – the 'ping' of a new email, a noise somewhere, the phone ringing – is enough to make us have to reset our concentration level. And let's face it, all of these are normal day-to-day stuff, particularly in today's open-plan offices. As much as such offices might encourage a more relaxed atmosphere, they have the opposite effect on our personal level of happiness. That's because people want to feel they're achieving something (and employers in particular have targets they want to meet), but the modern office environment massively affects the pace at which we work.

Even when we make a point of working in a quiet room, we still allow ourselves to be interrupted. Not only do we hear our email ping, but we then can't resist reading it or even responding before getting back to whatever we were doing before – at least until the next ping.

Similarly, if a customer or client calls we feel we have to drop everything to answer them straight away. But what if we were already with a client? In that case we'd think nothing of asking the second client if we could call them back.

To be really productive we need uninterrupted time. Helping your client to better organise their day to achieve this will lead to them getting more work done in less time.

To start, suggest they batch process emails, only loading them up once or twice per day to go through in one go. Similarly, they can batch process phone calls by getting someone to take a message. A standard response is all that's needed: "I'm afraid he/she's in a meeting until X o'clock. May I take a message?" (If they don't have anyone to filter their calls, they can outsource this. I explain a little more about this in 'Employ or Outsource' on page 106). Batch processing calls and emails will keep your client looking professional and help them improve productivity at the same time.

However, I don't want to suggest that I'm against technology. Remember how excited I was by my uncle's computer! In fact, I went on to be a computer programmer for many years, creating software packages that specifically supported businesses. It's just that technology – particularly social media – can hinder productivity if it's not used well. That said, there's some fantastic technology out there that could really help you or your clients.

A great exercise you can carry out to help them find the most suitable – I've used researchers in PeoplePerHour.com to do this, although I check out their results for myself before passing them on to clients – is to list a client's needs and then find the top ten pieces of cloud-based software to accommodate these.

Help them get their life back

When a person first sets up their own business, they often find themselves having to do everything from answering the phone, through to providing quotes, ordering stock, delivering on the product or service and invoicing.

As their business grows, however, they start to recruit people to take over some of these roles. The problem is, often they let go of the low-level tasks while keeping hold of the high-level ones. Why? Fear of losing control. In short, they're afraid that things won't get done as well. That they won't know what's going on. That jobs will slip through the net and standards will fall.

As they've put a lot of effort into building their business, this fear is understandable, but there are two problems here:

- They're working long hours and putting a strain on their health, friendships and family.

- The business isn't scalable. It will peak at the point where the business owner can no longer fit any more hours into their day.

Even a business that relies on its owner's unique skills will have some tasks which don't fall into this category. You can explore this with clients by using a great exercise that involves noting every single task they get involved in. Then, from that list, identify the ones they feel only they can do and try to understand why. Are they skilled in a specific art? Do they have so much knowledge about something that only they're equipped to do it? Although this may sometimes be the case, my guess is that many of the items on their lists could be delegated. (Not necessarily easily, but that's not the same as impossible).

A master chef's creative flare allows them to invent new food experiences. Their skills are unique. However, in order for them to do this, they can't also be the ones who produce that same experience over and over again for their restaurant customers. Instead, after they've come up with a new recipe, they train their team to reproduce it perfectly. The recipe is essentially a step-by-step system for others to follow.

By creating a system they're letting go. And, although learning to feel less protective of their skills can be difficult, teaching others to produce what they've created ultimately allows them to expand and share it with more people.

Once you've understood their feelings about each item on the list, go back through it to find out when they carry out each task. Usually you'll find they're trying to squeeze everything that isn't directly operational – quoting, invoicing, chasing debts and so on – into before 9am or after 5pm. And, as a one-person business, they'll usually be covering every role from marketing, sales and finance through to administration and customer service. (If they do expand and take on some help, often they'll find they've added people management to the list, rather than making their lives easier). Having to fulfil all these roles often means that they're fulfilling each of them insufficiently.

Earlier, I talked about the need to understand your clients' aspirations. Whatever these turned out to be, I'll bet that reducing their hours and taking more holidays came up in the discussion. However, although most people who go into business do so in order to work the hours they choose, the reality is that they end up working for the harshest boss in the world: themselves.

You can help them to change this.

I'd like to tell you a story about an accountant named Raj who joined AVN. It has an important message, but I need to give you a brief understanding of his journey with us first.

All journeys with AVN begin with quick wins. We help new members to generate significant returns early on, which enables them to not only cover their AVN investment, but also to reach a position where they can begin to invest money in their practice in order to grow.

Raj attended our training events and really began to embrace our concepts and methodologies. He changed his pricing structure. He began offering more value to his clients and he was starting to reap the rewards.

During this first stage, AVN focuses on the practice owner – in this case Raj – or a specific partner. The second phase to the AVN journey, however, involves systemising our client's practice, so that others in their team can be trained to cover some of the functions that previously fell on them.

To do this, we offer a shortcut by providing access to 'System Builder,' a cloud-based package we created especially for accountants. System Builder contains every system, form, checklist and script an accountancy practice might need. We carefully train and support clients in its use, tailoring the systems they choose to their specific business and circumstances.

Raj had gone through this training but had not yet begun to implement the systems within his practice. He'd reached the point where he could take a short break though, and decided to go over to India to see his family for a couple of weeks.

AVN has a team of practice growth experts who have regular check-ins with our members. We've found this helps them overcome any challenges they might be facing and keep their momentum going with the changes they're making. However, although Laura, one of our experts, had booked a phone call with Raj for about a week after his return, he didn't take the call. His receptionist said he wasn't available.

This seemed odd to Laura, as Raj had never missed a booked call before. Something important must have come up. She told the receptionist that she'd try again in a few days and left it at that.

A few days later she received the same response. She tried a few more times then decided to hold back a little and give him some space. She told his receptionist she'd call again in a month. A month later though, he still wouldn't take her call.

Eventually our finance team reported that Raj had missed a couple of payments. Laura brought this to my attention and ran through what had taken place. I said I'd try calling and, when I dialled the number, it was Raj who answered.

I asked him if everything was alright and explained why I was calling. What he told me next was terrible.

Whilst he'd been in India he'd been involved in a car crash which had left him in a coma for six weeks. When he came out of it and was released from hospital he came home to find that during his absence his employees (he'd had five) had tried to hold things together but couldn't. One by one they'd jumped ship and moved on.

He came back to a practice that had lost most of its clients. He was devastated. He'd spent years of hard work building his practice up and yet it couldn't cope without him.

He told me that never had the systems message been so apparent. If only he'd taken the time to get systems in place before he went away, the practice would have been able to continue in his absence.

If this happened to you, or to one of your clients, how long would your business last? Two or three months? Or two or three weeks?

It's because they enable business owners to delegate crucially important tasks that systems are so important. Once a system is in place, employees can follow it step-by-step, ensuring that the same consistently high standards are met every single time.

Systemising a business is an important task, but it's also a mammoth one. Not only do you need to create the systems, you also need to get your team to adopt the necessary mindset and to use them.

AVN accountants are able to help their business owners shortcut the process to some degree by providing them access to System Builder. Its generic set of systems cover:

- Finance.

- Marketing.

- Sales.

- Administration.

- Leadership.

- People.

- Customer Service.

This shortcuts the systemisation process. Every time a new business registers with System Builder its systems are replicated, which means the business is then free to tailor them to their individual preferences and focus on building the operational systems that are unique to their business.

When you work with clients to implement systems, it also helps if you break the task down. Start by identifying some of the easier areas – given your expertise, finance is often a good place to start – and then the key systems that need to be created within each of these areas. Once you've done this, you can map out the journey of system implementation they need to take across all aspects of their business.

However, before this can happen, they must establish buy-in from their employees. All of them will need training, and to understand the importance of systems, and all this must also be planned and mapped out.

A useful exercise to do here – and one which needs to involve everyone, so if you or your client have more than ten employees, divide them into smaller groups of a maximum of ten – is to find a large empty wall, then give everyone a pack of Post-it notes and ask each of them to write down every step they take when they make themselves a cup of coffee.

Once they've done this, get them to put their steps up on the wall, grouping the identical ones together. It'll then be easy to see that while some have used just three steps, others have written down a great many more.

Next, encourage them to get their system down to a maximum of seven steps. Explain that a system should never have too many steps. If it does, no one will follow it. On the other hand, too few steps will lead to gaps, or to each step being overcomplicated to accommodate all the information that's needed. Systems should always complement training, not replace the need for it.

This exercise will reveal a few things:

- Although everyone likes to do things their own way, in a business, this doesn't lead to consistency.

- Some people are more detailed than others and will want to list too much – rather than letting systems be an aide-memoire to training.

Sometimes, however, the biggest obstacle to the successful implementation of systems is when the business has multiple owners – an accountancy practice with more than one partner, for example. In my experience, many multi-partner firms are actually just independent sole practitioner firms run under one practice name. This can never bring consistency and should always be addressed first.

Employ or outsource?

Creating systems in a business doesn't mean that you have to employ someone to follow them.

We live in a time when we have access to millions of people around the world, many of whom can fulfill the roles you need for an incredibly small fee. Take answering the phone, for example. If you were to employ a receptionist you'd be paying a full-time wage. Undoubtedly you'd also give them jobs to do between calls, but they may not be sufficiently skilled to perform all of the functions you'd like them to.

Employing someone full-time means adding to your fixed-cost base. It also means that when they're ill, or on annual leave, you're back to square one.

Answering the telephone is one of the easiest things to outsource. Many companies simply charge a fee per call taken. They can answer as though they work for you, explain you're with a client and that you'll return the call between X and Y o'clock. In fact, they can take as much or as little information as you like. And you don't have to use an overseas company. These days, you're just as likely to find a local one. It also solves having to find sickness and holiday cover – the phone answering service deals with it all for you.

Using a phone answering service:

- Frees up some of the owner's time.

- Ensures that every call is answered – no more lost sales.

- Makes the business look more professional.

- Can have a massive impact on productivity.

Although at first your client might not like the idea of paying someone to answer the phone when they can do it themselves, or are unsure about trusting another business to represent their own, what's the opportunity cost? When a business owner takes a call they have to stop whatever else they're doing. They may be driving and unable to fully concentrate. They may have been trying to complete an important job and become irritated by a prospective customer asking lots of questions. Or, worse still, they may have promised to call back, jotted the number down on a bit of paper and then lost it. Ask your client to think about how much in lost sales it might be costing them to answer the phone themselves.

How many situations do we outsource without even thinking about it? Creating a website is an obvious one. Using a graphic designer for letterheads is another. Getting the photocopier fixed, a third. Going through your client's entire list of functions and finding alternative ways to get them done is one of the simplest and best ways to free up their time.

At this point, as their accountant, you're likely to spot some functions that your firm can provide. Many accountants offer a debt-collecting service, for example. How valuable might that be to clients who only have time to chase debts outside their 9-5 work? At times when the odds are that the debtor's business is closed, meaning all they can do is leave an answerphone message.

That's why having these types of discussion with clients is so valuable – it can often lead to additional work. In general, I use the following rule of thumb: If it's repetitive work then a system can be created and it can be outsourced.

Create a form to go through with your client with these headings:

- Function.

- Role.

- When.

- Repetitive.

- Action.

An action could be to systemise the process, it could be to stop doing it as it's just not that important in the grand scheme of things or has little impact. The point is to have a discussion and really understand each function and whether it should be done and by whom.

Decide an action for every function listed and see how many functions can be taken off the shoulders of your client. Yes, this will cost, but what's the opportunity cost? What's the cost to their personal life? Can they justify taking a hit in income if it means they can spend more time with their family? (If they free up some time and reduce their stress levels, they'll be able to). The most likely result though is that the changes will quickly start to generate work and soon be paying for themselves – and then some!

The support you can bring

Great ideas will never be implemented as effectively without the help, encouragement, nagging and accountability you can provide.

How much support you choose to deliver will of course impact on your time and so it's only fair that you allow your client to choose how much support they want to pay for.

In Part 4 we're going to pull everything together in to a structured business growth programme to make it easier to promote to your clients as a package. In fact, we're going to assemble a three tier package in order to offer your clients a choice about how much help and support they want. More on that in Part 4, but for now it's a good idea for you to consider just how much support you could give if somebody wanted the maximum amount you could (and would be prepared to offer). Don't worry about the fees right now, just consider the possibilities.

So what might you build into your programme in terms of support? Although I'll list a few suggestions below, I recommend you add to them. (You don't have to include them all every time, but it's always good to consider all the options. Think of all the ways you could support people, even if right now they seem impractical).

- After each session you could produce a report summarising your discussion and listing the actions agreed with dates and who's been allocated to do them.

- You could build in regular follow-up phone calls/emails/texts.

- You, or someone in your team, could go to your client's office once a week to help them implement some of the actions, such as creating systems for important activities, by shadowing the person carrying out those actions.

- You could offer ongoing accountability sessions for X months.

What other ways could you add value by helping your client implement the actions they've agreed to?

Add them to the list above.

Part 4
Start Really Making A Positive Difference To Clients

Developing a packaged product around consulting

How often have you given great business advice to a client but felt that you couldn't really charge as it just came up in conversation? Do you feel that some of your clients exploit your knowledge? Are they happy to soak it up like a sponge but don't really seem to appreciate it – or you?

We don't always value stuff that's free.

Of course sometimes it's necessary to provide things for free, particularly if this forms part of a larger strategy. Demonstrating knowledge in a certain area builds your credibility. However, separating what you're prepared to give away for free, from what you'll deliver only as part of a paid-for product can be difficult.

It's often even harder these days as so much information is freely available. Many of the questions a client asks could simply be entered into Google. Luckily though, it's more convenient for them to ask you than to have to trawl through the varying quality of the millions of responses that would throw up.

In addition, Google won't take them through a thought provoking journey of exploration as to why they're running their business, what their dreams are, formulating ideas and actions which fit with their dreams, values and beliefs. Only another human being can do that.

The Internet contains thousands of consultants trying to sell their 'Three-Step Formula to Business Success' or their 'Seven-Step Formula to Making Millions'.

I'm sure some of the formulas they put forward are effective but – as many of those consultants are the first to admit – there's no such thing as an easy ride when it comes to success. And what does success mean anyway? It's subjective – which means it's different for everyone.

There's nothing wrong with formulas and systems – I've shared a few in this book – the problems arise when business owners think they'll lead to instant results. And that's why selling books with titles such as X-Step Formulas works, because people want shortcuts. They want to take as few steps as possible to get to where they want to be. They like the sound of a finite journey. It allows them to think, "Seven steps? That shouldn't take long at all!"

We all know, however, that the reality is different; very few of the people who buy these formulas get results. Why? Because they lack accountability, encouragement, support and help that's specifically tailored to their requirements.

Online formulas can only ever be generic. They can't help drill down to the root of the problem, provoke thoughts on the best solutions, or help make them happen.

I'm not saying they don't help at all, but the bottom line is you can't beat working one-to-one with someone. This doesn't mean that you don't need a programme at all though. It's important to come up with one as it suggests there's an end in sight. And – and this is the part you'll probably find most unnerving – you need to prove its value by offering a money-back guarantee if a client isn't satisfied by the time it ends. (I'll go into more detail about this later, but for now, you just need to know that it's vital if potential clients are to take the plunge).

In Part 2 of this book under the heading of 'A coach? A mentor? or a consultant?' I shared an analogy about a sick patient visiting the doctors who after an initial consultation prescribed a course of action (presumably antibiotics in this case) so that the patient would get better.

Sometimes people want to know that a shorter term solution is available to them where they can see some instant results.

I recommend that you develop a programme. In fact, I recommend that you develop three programmes in order to provide choice to your clients.

Many people like to have a choice about the product, or in this case programme, they're going to purchase. They will shop around and obtain three prices. However, if you can present three options this meets the need to obtain the three prices.

Come up with an all singing, all dancing programme, where you're putting in a lot of your time to work more closely and support your client. Perhaps the programme covers a lot of content and consists of many sessions spread over a period of time.

Let's call that your premium package.

From that create a standard and an elite version. You may prefer to use terms like Gold, Silver, Bronze or 5 Star, 4 Star, 3 Star. As long as they're differentiated in such a way that it's clear that one is better than the other, that's fine.

At the back of this book are some resources for you. Appendix 1 takes you through the process of creating a brochure. Largely this is a repeat of the steps I detail in 'Getting – and getting more from – customers' and specifically item 3 of that section entitled 'Converting leads into customers' on page 90. Although I've repeated the steps, I've included more detail about the type of content you could consider and include in a brochure to help you promote business improvement sessions. I recommend that you work through that in Appendix 1. The process of creating the brochure will ensure that you've considered important aspects such as the typical business problems you're aware of and want to fix as well as designing your three tiered packages.

Whilst I don't recommend that you print your fees in your brochure as these are more subject to change, it's important you know what you're going to charge for each of the sessions you plan to deliver.

In addition, It's advisable not to share the fees until you've showed the potential impact your sessions could have on a client's business. Quoting a price without showing how low that price is compared to the increased profits they stand to make is an opportunity missed and unlikely to be received with optimism. Show the possibilities first. I'll walk you through the process shortly.

What's it worth? Pricing your product

You have two main options: fixed fee or value pricing.

Although most accountants have shifted from billing by the hour to a fixed-fee approach, many simply estimate the amount of hours they think a job will take and give a price based on that.

I'm not a fan of using this model because, in many if not most cases, basing a fee on an hourly rate is leaving money on the table, undervaluing yourself and your experience. That said, if you prefer to take this approach, at the very least you need to consider the following...

Use your typical charge-out rate for each session. These ought to be around two to three hours in length and accommodate both pre-session prep and post-session support. Build in some time for nagging and then work out a fixed price from this for each of your service levels.

Let's say this gives you something along the following lines:

Gold service	£30,000
Silver service	£8,000
Bronze service	£600

This approach will work. It's crystal clear for you and for your client and you've priced the options according to the level of support and number of sessions you'll deliver.

The downside is, however, that it often leaves money you could be earning on the table.

To avoid this, I'd suggest you use value pricing.

As there are many ways to value price your services, I'm not going to run through them all in this book right now.

One common approach however is to agree a fee that's a percentage of your success.

If, for example, I stated that I could take your business from a £1m turnover to £10m, and would only charge 10% of the upside, would that be worth it to you?

Or if I could demonstrate that implementing some of the ideas we come up with has the potential to increase your profits by over £200,000 in the next 12 months – that's a million pounds over the next five years – would you be happy for us to work to a percentage of success payment of 15%?

Work out the numbers that matter to your client and then, by asking them what it would be worth to them to achieve those numbers, come up with a suggested percentage of the value and state it with confidence. Clearly this method is results based and your client may not be a great action taker. Use your judgement as to whether or not it's better to agree a fixed fee or a value based fee depending on your client. It's worth bearing in mind though that if you stand to earn a large success fee it's in your interest to pester your client more to take action which in turn will benefit them and you.

A third option might be to offer a fixed-fee payment plus a bonus based on your success e.g. £8,000 + 5% of the increase in profit.

The concept of top-down pricing

You're going to come up with three service levels with a fee for each. The top level will be the premium fee and the lowest level the smallest fee.

Many people make the mistake of talking through the lowest service offering first and then trying to upsell. This is a mistake.

When you price your service, always start with the highest-level. Talk your client through it, explaining the benefits of everything it consists of – even if you don't believe for a minute they'll go for it. Why? Because:

- It stops you making assumptions about your clients.

- Even if they don't go for it themselves, they might share the information with others.

- When you move to the middle service level, you'll be explaining what they're not going to get if they go for that level compared to the higher lever. No one likes to feel they're missing out on something, so often this will encourage them to go for the higher option.

Let me share a story that's often used to explain how top-down pricing works.

A man walks in to a menswear shop to buy a suit. He's going for an important interview and wants to look great.

As he enters he's approached by an assistant who offers to help him find the right suit and leads him over to a long rack on which there are about 20 suits, ranging from the cheapest on the left to the most expensive on the right.

Although the man had specified he didn't want to spend too much, the assistant takes him to the suits on the right, the most expensive ones, first.

The assistant then begins to describe the quality of the first suit, its stitching, its cut, explaining the benefits of each of these – the first impression wearing such a suit will give, the comfort and so on. However, when the assistant reveals the price the man explains that it's outside his budget.

Rather than jump to the cheaper end of the rack, the assistant moves to the next suit down where he repeats the process. This time, though, he compares the quality of the slightly cheaper suit to the more expensive one. Although it's slightly lower quality than the first one, however, he stresses that it will still give a good impression.

Although the man again explains that even this price is outside his budget, you can tell it's hurting. He really wants to make the best impression he can. He wants to look professional and he certainly doesn't want to appear in a cheap-looking suit.

At this point the assistant takes him to the third suit and repeats the process yet again. This time when he reveals the price the man agrees to purchase it. Although it's still much more expensive than he'd intended, he recognises he needs to look professional, makes the additional investment and walks away looking and feeling fantastic.

The assistant could easily have taken the man to the cheapest suit first. He could have explained the quality, stitching and cut in exactly the same way and the man may well have gone straight for it. If the assistant had then attempted to upsell the next suit along, explaining its superiority, there's no guarantee he would have succeeded – even the best salesman or woman finds upselling harder than a top-down technique. Plus, the customer would have left feeling he'd received the hard-sell.

And that's why great sales representatives always use the top-down approach.

Many of the accountants I work with fear taking the top-down pricing approach because they pre-judge clients, either assuming they can't afford something or that they're price sensitive. The best way to know if someone is price sensitive or not is to look at the clothes they're wearing or the car they drive. If they really are price sensitive, then the cheapest clothes or car will be sufficient. But how often is that the case? People buy top-brand cars not because they're more reliable or safer – even if these are the reasons they give. They purchase them for emotional reasons. They want to look good. They want the sense of status it gives them.

In fact, most people's buying decisions are based more on emotions than rationale, which means – where possible – you should describe the benefits of your product or service in terms of feelings of gain or loss of pain.

Earlier I gave an example fee of £30,000 for your top-level service. If you were to take a look at your client's accounts, understand how many hours they work and how high their stress levels are, and then look at the potential impact on their business and personal life of some marginal gains here and there, what do you think this might be worth to them? To get their life back and still have a business that funds that life?

You can make that difference to your client. I know because I've seen it done countless times by other accountants who've taken the plunge and offered business growth sessions to clients in the way I've described. And once you have that belief in the difference you can make, you're less likely to crash your price. There are, however, several other reasons why you shouldn't, which I'll now run through below.

Why you should never crash the price

I'm sure you've had a client challenge you on price. Many people thrive on feeling that they're getting a better deal and will challenge any price you offer. Sadly, in response, many people crash their price almost straight away. The client leaves feeling they've got a good deal and you leave feeling a bit miffed overall, but still pleased that you got the work.

The problem is that because you crashed your price so easily, the client assumes that you must have been attempting to rip them off in the first place. Not only that, but they then tell others, who also start to challenge you. In the end, no one values your time or the services you offer. So please never crash your price.

Instead, the next time someone challenges you on price, ask them what they'd like you to remove from the package to bring it down to their budget. It'll send out a clear message that you value your time and the service or product you provide. If they want to pay less, then they'll get less in return.

Apple, for example, are great at this. Have you ever known them to give a discount on their product? Instead, they simply offer you the next model down – usually adding 'Although it won't allow you to store as many photographs of course.'

Do you remember how in the section on creating the perfect brochure I explained the importance of listing the benefits of each feature? And how you should always include the overall benefit of your product or service as well as the individual benefits of each of its features?

If your price isn't being accepted it means you're not selling the value of your product or service sufficiently well. Many people fail to do this because they focus on the features rather than the benefits, or fail to base the benefits on emotional as well as rational gains.

The bottom-up approach

Earlier I discussed how a top-down approach is more likely to lead to a great sale. However, if your client does plump for the bottom or middle tier then you still have the option to upgrade them. You can do this – once it's completed – by asking if they got value from the sessions. Assuming they answer yes, ask if they'd like to upgrade to the next level in order to continue getting the same great value.

(I wouldn't mention this option during the sales process though, otherwise people might only go for the bottom option with a view to upgrading after each session if they feel they've got value).

Guarantees

Investing in a product or service without any real knowledge that it's going to work is a hefty decision to make.

That's why offering a money-back guarantee will significantly increase your conversion rate.

That said, I'm not suggesting that at the end of the programme you ask your client if they feel they've got value and if not you should give them every single penny back. That would be unfair.

However many great ideas you and your client come up with, the onus to implement them lies entirely in their hands. And sadly, no matter how much you try to hold them to account, you can never guarantee that they will.

There are many things you can guarantee, but guaranteeing the outcome isn't something I would suggest you do. I recommend that you guarantee value from each session. Divide the fee by the number of session that you will delivering and guarantee that proportion. This will limit any guarantee trigger amount.

To demonstrate the value in each session, what you can do is calculate the potential impact of each idea you discuss – as well as their combined impact – and then extrapolate this up to show the additional profits your client could gain over a five-year period.

By doing this you're demonstrating the value of your conversations. The impact is based on your client's judgement rather than you implying it. i.e. this idea could potentially increase my sales by 2%'. Your job is to do the math in terms of combining the impact of all ideas discussed and extrapolate them.

Often the ideas discussed in just one session could have a huge impact on the bottom line. Drilling down in to what your client might do with this additional income will lead to the benefits – both emotional and financial – being better appreciated too. So the best time to ask a client if they've had value from the session is at this point.

As suggested, implement the guarantee per session. At the end of each one, make sure you demonstrate the benefits of the actions you've discussed. Then ask if they've had value and, if not, would they like to trigger the guarantee.

As long as you've made the value clear to them, there's no reason why they should. In fact, I've never yet heard of a guarantee being triggered.

In the unlikely event it were though, you'd probably already be aware that the session hadn't been entirely successful. And, if that were the case, you could ask whether – as you don't feel you've given sufficient value – they'd like their money back or another session instead.

In the even more unlikely event that you feel a client has triggered the guarantee unfairly, I'd suggest honouring your guarantee by returning their money, but discontinuing the programme.

Although you can never guarantee clients will implement your ideas, it's in your interests for them to do so. Not only will they see the results, leading to raving testimonials and referrals, but they'll also be in a much better place as a result of the difference you've made.

The more you can persuade clients to buy into an idea by helping them to formulate it, the higher the chance of implementing. The more you can draw out its emotional benefits, the higher the chance of implementing. The more you can hold clients to account, the higher the chance of implementing.

How to progress to a consulting session

I've shared tips and techniques you can use to have great business growth conversations with clients and given you the foundations to create a packaged product with a brochure to complement it. Let's now walk through the steps needed to effectively promote and then deliver consulting sessions.

Who should you approach?

If you remember my explanation of how to grade your client base – where A's are both profitable and great people, and D's are the least profitable and often difficult – you may feel it's best to start with your C or D clients. That way, if things don't work out, it's not so bad if you lose them.

In fact, the best clients to approach are your A's. That's because they're already advocates and will be much more open to you working with them in this way. They'll also be more forgiving if things don't quite go to plan and will really appreciate you asking them.

D's, meanwhile, often don't share the same values as you. They may be a D because they've negotiated your fee down in the first place, which means they're less interested in the value you can deliver and more interested in getting their accounts done at rock-bottom prices. Your D clients will also be the ones who give you and your team the hardest time and are most likely to trigger the guarantee.

My firm recommendation then is that you approach your best client first and ask them if they'd be willing to participate in your programme.

A script to get your first client

The script below deliberately uses the word pilot. This helps to clarify that the programme is new, exclusive and possibly still a little rough around the edges and – because you've set up this expectation – clients are likely to be more forgiving as a result.

The script also suggests you offer the programme for free. Despite my earlier comments about how important it is that you charge a fee, it's also important to consider the first two or even three sessions as training to build up your confidence, competence and credibility – especially if you've never done anything like this before.

"Dave, we've been developing an exciting new business-growth programme. It pulls together my/our experience working with hundreds of businesses in different sectors, seeing what works and what doesn't – and we're now starting to pilot it.

Once we roll it out it will be a £8,000 process called XXXXXXX. It's designed to give businesses the edge, to make them more successful and profitable, and to help business owners like yourself get from where you are to where you want to be.

But I'd like to make a suggestion. I'd like to cover that £8000 from my budget – so that you can enjoy all the benefits of the programme without it costing you a penny.

This means you'll get £8,000 worth of value and help for FREE. Does that sound as good an idea to you as it does to me? Great. All I ask in return is that:

- *You're kind to me since, as I say, we're still piloting the programme.*

- *You offer constructive feedback so that we can make the process even more valuable for the next business.*

- *You provide a testimonial and case study at the end if you're as delighted with the process as I know you will be.*

Does that seem fair? Great, let's put a date to start in our diaries."

I know this script works because we give it to AVN members so they can roll this service out to their clients. It's important that you use it wisely, however, and only offer the programme for free to your first two or three clients.

If you're a perfectionist you'll never feel completely ready to start charging. But after the first two or three clients you'll already have seen the difference you can make, so my advice is to perfect your skills through hands-on experience and continue to tweak your approach along the way.

At the end of each pilot session, make sure you capture a short video testimonial from your client. Did they find the process valuable? Why? Would they recommend the session to others?

It's unlikely you'll have completed your brochure by this point, so the pilot sessions can also help you with this – allowing you to fine tune the benefits of what you offer and provide testimonials and case studies.

Moving on to paying clients

Although the script is a great way to help you find clients to pilot your service for free, it's unlikely to help you establish paid work.

This means that you need another way to promote your business advisory work. From my experience, one of the best methods is to produce really valuable reports which help clients better understand their numbers and – even more importantly – the strengths and weaknesses of their business and where their best opportunities lie.

A shortcut to powerful reports
Although I'm sure you could create a good one yourself, at AVN we provide tools to help you produce incredibly powerful and valuable reports with very little effort. Our BenchMark product,

for example, enables you to compare the business you're working with to similar ones throughout the country, using key attributes to show exactly where your client stands in comparison to his or her competitors – anonymously of course.

I suspect you've come across clients who've begun to accept and rationalise their circumstances, who say, for example, "Yes, my debtor days are very high, but to be honest that's just the way it is in my type of business." However, by showing – let's say – that their competitors have on average 40 debtor days compared to their 120, not only can you prove to them that this figure can be improved upon, you can also use it as a lead in to having a meaningful discussion about how they might make it happen. (And the number of debtor days is just an example. Our BenchMark report includes a breakdown of many other key attributes and makes some suggestions on how to improve these).

Below is an example of a report:

One Page Performance Improvement Plan				

Where are you now			Where you want to be	How you get there
Your key numbers		Which ranks you	Your targets	Your action plan
Sales growth	14.3%		**Sales** – What would you like your sales growth and margin of safety to be? NB: Improving your sales growth to match the upper quartile – i.e. to 25.0% – will add £37,108 in extra profit.	**Sales** – As a first step calculate the impact of working on each of the key sales drivers, i.e. getting more sales leads, converting more sales leads, keeping customers for longer, selling more to each customer and selling more often.
Margin of safety	30.0%			
Gross margin	35.0%			
Operating margin	10.5%		**Profit** – What would you like your profits to be? NB: Improving your gross margin to match the upper quartile – i.e. to 79.9% – will add £109,600 in extra profit.	**Profit** – As a first step focus on pricing – since pricing is often the biggest single factor driving the profitability of many businesses. Look at the sales mix by carrying out gross margin analysis by customer and/or product group. Review costs control. And investigate process inefficiencies.
Net profit margin	10.5%			
Growth in net profit	50.0%			
Sales per £ of employee costs	£2.14		**People costs and productivity** – What would you like your average employee costs, sales per employee, sales per £ of employee costs and profit per employee to be? NB: Improving your sales per £ of employee costs to match the upper quartile – i.e. to £2.46 – will add £21,309 in extra profit.	**People costs and productivity** – Systems are the key to productivity and efficiency. Review the systems and processes. Identify areas of waste and inefficiency. Map out more effective systems and document them. Involve the team in creating better systems. And then train the team in following the business systems and processes.
Average employee costs	£45,750			
Sales per employee	£100,045			
Profit per employee	£10,500			
Asset turnover	4.04		**Assets** – What would you like your asset turnover, debtor days, stock days and debtors to total asset ratio to be? NB: Improving your asset turnover by 10% – i.e. to 4.44 – will add £26,000 in extra profit. Improving your stock days to match the upper quartile – i.e. to 5.1 days – will add £14,271 to the amount of cash you have in the bank. And improving your debtor days by 10% – i.e. to 1.7 days – will add £28,208 to the amount of cash you have in the bank.	**Assets** – As a first step, identify ways of getting paid on time, in full, every time. Then create the operational and financial systems you need to reduce debtors, work in progress and stock.
Stock days	5.82			
Debtor days	1.92			**Cash and gearing** – Explore refinancing options, and consider invoice discounting, factoring and asset finance. Also, review your credit control systems and processes for paying suppliers, and renegotiate the interest paid on borrowing. And avoid nasty surprises by producing regular high quality cash flow forecasts.
Debtors to total assets	2.12			
Current ratio	3.83			
Quick ratio	3.17			
Interest cover	0		**Return on investment** – What would you like your return on investment to be? NB: Improving your return on investment to match the upper quartile – i.e. to 49.1% – will add £94,678 in extra profit.	**Return on investment** – Much of the above will have a big impact on your return on investment. What else can you do?
Return on investment	42.4%			
Return on capital employed	45.2%			

©AVN 2014

The beauty of a report like this is that it reveals strengths and weaknesses at a glance. However, we advise AVN members never to simply send their report with the accounts, but to use it as a conversational tool during meetings. This helps to raise their credibility and allows them to ask clients if they'd like their help in improving any of these areas.

If you'd like to learn more about the types of tools AVN provide, and how to gain access to them go to:
www.improveyourpractice.co.uk

Alternatively, at the beginning of Part 3 there's a section on page 74 entitled 'What are the numbers that matter?'

This is an incredibly effective 'in.' Go through this process with a client, really seek to understand the numbers that matter, why they're important, identify the gaps between now and the desired future and show them the possibilities for closing the gaps. The best way to do this is to explore some of the Sales Growth Drivers and quantify the potential of each idea explored. Go through this with them in detail and for free.

Put together some actions they could take to begin seeing some of those benefits and ask them if they'd like help.

When they enquire what that help consists of, go through the brochure with them, using it as a guide for your sales script. Talk through the problems that you're aware your customers typically experience. One of those problems is likely to be that they're so busy running their business and working in it that they don't get the chance to step back and make the all-important necessary changes. Go through how you can help them with regular sessions, with each session leading to developing ways to reduce their time working 'in' the business to 'on' it which typically means less hours in general and greater income too. Explain how you can help them map out step by step how they're going to implement each idea and run through your support process.

Remember to use the top-down pricing principle explained on page 118.

Emphasise the guarantee (page 122), it's incredibly powerful and reverses the risk from their side.

And don't be afraid to ask them if they'd like to go ahead and be ready to sign them up. Don't make the mistake many people make in that they go through all of this process and then simply leave it for someone to go away and think about it. It's important to strike whilst the iron is hot and after you've contrasted your fee against the potential impact on their business from a relatively brief exploratory review. Asking if they'd like to go ahead isn't a strong close. Their response may well be that they need to think about it. Quite likely though, they'll sign up there and then, especially as there's no risk with the comfort of the guarantee.

Delivering a powerful consulting session

Now I've shared these three ways to help you promote your consulting programme, let's take a look at how you might deliver the sessions.

Preparing
Always do as much preparation as you can prior to each session.

Personally, I enjoy listening to audio books – it seems to trigger the business part of my brain and so when I'm on my way to visit a client I tend to listen to a business audio book. It helps me to prepare mentally.

With the exception of the operational side of their business, most of the challenges your clients face will be generic: sales, marketing, prioritising and so on. That being said, it never hurts to research their sector, so carry out an Internet search of the top ten mistakes made, the top ten tips or the top ten challenges. This will help you build up some ideas that are pertinent to their particular business. Dropped in to your conversations, they might help get other ideas flowing.

Remember your client probably hasn't got time to research solutions themselves. At most they may have invested in a quick-fix solution they found on the Internet, but the chances are this wasn't focused on their specific industry.

Take another look at my 'What to focus on' chapter to remind you of the different areas you can explore with your client and to ascertain how they're doing in each of these.

If you have a team of people, carry out a quick brainstorm session. Ask them to think about things they've seen other clients do – whether it's great customer service, innovative lead-generation techniques, or even a particularly efficient way to run their business.

How to structure your sessions

Below is a rough guide as to how I run through a session, but don't forget to use your judgement – sometimes you need to adapt the order.

Highlights
What great things have happened since the last session or over the past few weeks? Asking this helps to shift your client to a more positive frame of mind. Although it can be difficult for them to come up with positives to start with, pursue it for a while to see what you can tease out of them. Anything that will make them sit up straight and smile helps.

Progress update
What progress have they made on the actions from the previous session? If the answer's very little, what got in the way? How could they overcome this? Take a look at the original numbers you helped them to come up with, the numbers that matter to them. How have these been affected so far? Keep coming back to these.

Topics for the day
The first session should focus on the big picture. Even if you don't get as far as their vision and goals, make sure you understand where they're at and what fires they're currently fighting. It's okay to be the consultant at this point, to make recommendations

and to explore alternatives with them. If they're juggling lots of balls, use the two matrices and the table to list out the stuff they're doing to help them prioritise. Look at their productivity and try to eliminate distractions so they can focus. Find out if they can work from home one day – or even one morning – per week to lock themselves away and get things done.

Help them move to a position where they can focus on quadrant 2 rather than quadrant 1 items, to where they're implementing ideas that will make their business better. In subsequent sessions, use your judgement as to which of my other suggestions you should focus on. (Although – because the potential impact is so high, and because most businesses fail due to poor sales – I'd suggest you return to the sales growth drivers in every session).

Actions to take away
During the session write down all the ideas mentioned. Towards the end, turn these in to next-step actions with your client and decide when they should be implemented. Remember: the way actions are agreed upon has a huge impact on whether or not they're implemented.

Want some help with that?

If your client is struggling, could you help in some way? Do they need to create systems? Do they need to develop their business plan? Or chase up some debt? If so, it's important that you work out an appropriate fee and offer that service in the form of an extra work order rather than simply feeling obliged to go that extra mile which often means you'll lose out financially and risk becoming taken for granted.

It's important to capture case studies from your clients. The reason for inviting the first client to run through this process for free is twofold, to build up your confidence and skill and also to capture evidence that this stuff works.

Go through Appendix 2 – How to capture great case studies.

Ask for referrals

I've covered the principles of asking for referrals in 'Getting more leads' on page 89.

Show gratitude to anyone who gives you a referral – it doesn't have to be huge. Sometimes just a thank-you card will suffice, or perhaps a bottle of Champagne. This will encourage more referrals.

We've now covered promoting and delivering your consulting programme. However, although this will bring in significant fees, as a one-off sale it won't improve your gross recurring-fee income. In Part 5, we'll address how you can significantly increase your year-on-year income.

Part 5
Creating
Recurring Income

Accountants I've worked with who've embraced this change work the hours they choose, make a huge difference to their clients and enjoy stress-free, high-income lifestyles. You can, too, but not if you're having to continually sell one-off consulting programmes.

In this final section, I'll show you how to make generating new work easier as well as how to retain regular income by changing the way you work with clients.

Recall the section of this book entitled 'The change journey' on page 51.

Part 4 is intended to take a client through to being committed and taking action but the programme you've worked through with your client is for a finite period. Whether it's a half-day session or a 12 month programme, it will come to an end. It's important to continue to support your client on an ongoing basis in order to ensure they're able to continue to accommodate and evaluate the changes they're making.

Offering clients an ongoing monthly or quarterly meetings – either in the form of a board meeting at which you play the role of both non-executive and Finance Director or purly as ongoing consulting sessions – is a great way to help them keep the process of change going, while also generating ongoing recurring fee income for yourself.

Use the 'numbers that matter' sheet to maintain focus in these meetings. Update these and bring them to every meeting. At AVN we provide our accountants with a OnePage Plan™ template and training on how to produce them in the most effective way, which consists of not more than 15 - 20 metrics in order to prevent 'analysis paralysis.'

Separate these numbers – which should be the business' key performance indicators (KPIs) – into lag indicators and lead indicators and place the lag indicators at the top of the page. These are the key results, the consequence of what's been done in the past. Lag indicators – profit, revenue etc. – are easy to measure but difficult to change.

As you move down the page, progress towards the lead indicators, the underlying success drivers. These are more difficult to measure but easier to change. Customer happiness, for example, is often a great KPI because if customers are happy they'll continue to buy and to recommend you to others. If they're not, it's a great opportunity to talk to them and learn how to make the business better.

Team happiness is similar. An unhappy team affects customer service, production and sales. Talking to them to find out what would make them feel more motivated is a morale-raiser in itself and working to improve this will have a positive impact on financial performance.

Other indicators you might want to measure include sales drivers and cost and cash drivers. Sales drivers might consist of sales enquiries generated, conversion rate and average customer spend. While cost and cash drivers might include debtor days and exhibition costs.

Place the business' main goal at the bottom of the page as a reminder that everything they do should strive towards this.

Opposite is an example of an AVN OnePage Plan™

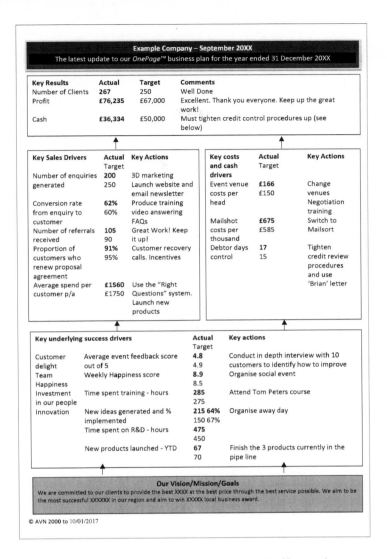

Example Company – September 20XX
The latest update to our *OnePage™* business plan for the year ended 31 December 20XX

Key Results	Actual	Target	Comments
Number of Clients	267	250	Well Done
Profit	£76,235	£67,000	Excellent. Thank you everyone. Keep up the great work!
Cash	£36,334	£50,000	Must tighten credit control procedures up (see below)

Key Sales Drivers	Actual Target	Key Actions
Number of enquiries generated	200 250	3D marketing Launch website and email newsletter
Conversion rate from enquiry to customer	62% 60%	Produce training video answering FAQs
Number of referrals received	105 90	Great Work! Keep it up!
Proportion of customers who renew proposal agreement	91% 95%	Customer recovery calls. Incentives
Average spend per customer p/a	£1560 £1750	Use the "Right Questions" system. Launch new products

Key costs and cash drivers	Actual Target	Key Actions
Event venue costs per head	£166 £150	Change venues Negotiation training
Mailshot costs per thousand	£675 £585	Switch to Mailsort
Debtor days control	17 15	Tighten credit review procedures and use 'Brian' letter

Key underlying success drivers		Actual Target	Key actions
Customer delight	Average event feedback score out of 5	4.8 4.9	Conduct in depth interview with 10 customers to identify how to improve
Team Happiness	Weekly Happiness score	8.9 8.5	Organise social event
Investment in our people	Time spent training - hours	285 275	Attend Tom Peters course
Innovation	New ideas generated and % implemented	215 64% 150 67%	Organise away day
	Time spent on R&D - hours	475 450	
	New products launched - YTD	67 70	Finish the 3 products currently in the pipe line

Our Vision/Mission/Goals
We are committed to our clients to provide the best XXXX at the best price through the best service possible. We aim to be the most successful XXXXXX in our region and aim to win XXXXX local business award.

© AVN 2000 to 10/01/2017

Start to work more closely with clients through offering this type of service and your gross recurring income will build and build.

Leverage

The final challenge when following my advice leads to so much success that you start to run out of time. Nothing I've shared so far can't be shared with others in your team. They might have less experience than you, but their ability to ask great questions, their knowledge and their skill with numbers make them excellent candidates to help you provide these services to more people.

Some AVN accountants, for example, charge a premium to deliver the programme or the ongoing board meetings themselves, while charging a slightly lower fee if one of their senior team members does so. Others might start the process off, but bring one of their team along to the early sessions so that – at a suitable point – they can hand the remaining sessions over to them. Both approaches leave you free to continue to build a profitable business rather than purely becoming a self-employed coach.

Another way to leverage the programme is to deliver group sessions, which allows you to earn significantly more for the same amount of time a one-to-one session would take. Essentially you follow the same process, but with a group. In addition, a group of business owners will all bring something different to the table and you might find that your input can be reduced to asking the great questions and offering recommendations.

You can even do this online by facilitating video-based group coaching sessions. As location is no longer important, not only does this significantly increase the number of your potential clients, it also means business owners from the same industry will be more willing to share best practice as they're less likely to see other members of the group as competitors.

Although your fee for video-based sessions will be less, the group can be considerably larger to include people who generally prefer to listen and only make the occasional contribution. In addition, a six-monthly or annual meet-up in person makes for a great day

– and don't forget it's always worth including a meeting in the hotel bar the night before!

Sadly, despite being all-too aware that the world of the traditional accountant is crashing around them, many people won't embark on the journey I suggest in this book. Many won't even step outside their comfort zone to try. But I implore you not to be one of them.

If you need further encouragement to get started, my YouTube channel (**www.youtube.com/c/AVNChangingtheNumbers**) includes lots of additional techniques and titbits you can either implement within your practice or use with clients in the future.

Fake it 'till you make it

I'd like to leave you with one final thought. Research shows that acting like the person you want to be significantly increases your chances of becoming that person. So shoulders back, chin up – and go make a difference!

Appendix 1 – Creating a brochure to showcase your product

In 'Converting leads into customers' I explained my nine-step process to creating a great brochure. Now, as an exercise to help you put together your package, gain clarity over the benefits you can bring and the support and service levels you can offer, I'd like to take you through creating your brochure.

And, if you're wondering why I don't just include a template you can use, it's because it's crucial that you use words which are most important to you personally. That way, you'll appeal to the type of client you'll be able to help the most. Your values and beliefs will come through if you write the brochure yourself – particularly if you convey your emotions. People relate to emotions.

Step 1. Describe the pain/problem/challenge
The first step is to show clients that not only do you understand their pain and the challenges they face, but that you can help them overcome these.

Where are your clients right now? Whatever the business, areas that come up time and time again are lack of time and money – both of which are the effects of multiple causes. So rather than detail these, elaborate on their consequences. Paint a picture of a life that doesn't have enough time: time to grow the business, time to spend with loved ones, time to spend doing the things they'd like to do outside of running their business.

Now take a few minutes to write a list of all the mistakes that you see business owners make, and all the challenges you see them face. Aim for 30 at least. The more you can come up with, the better your chance of filtering out the top three.

Step 2. Describe the big-picture benefits of removing that pain
Start by flipping everything you just listed for their pain. Then add any other benefits you can think of – but be careful to keep this attainable.

What types of client do you work with? What types of business do they run? What might a more enjoyable and successful business look like for them?

What does success mean to you?

Success is subjective. It means something different to everyone. Take a few minutes to really think about what it means to you and then write it down. (This can simply be some one-liners, or a longer description of an ideal time in the future. It's up to you).

You can't read your clients' minds, but you can paint a picture of what success looks like to you.

As an example, let me briefly share with you what success means to me personally.

It boils down to 3 things....

- I'm loving what I do and that I'm making a difference.

- I'm able to make great lifestyle choices.

- I'm have financial security.

And to elaborate...

In my early career years I saw a real difference between work and life. I was never a 'tools down at 5pm' type of person and have always worked over and above, but I always differentiated life and work. Now there's no difference, I'm passionate about what I do and I'm always thinking about how I can positively affect more lives.

Through my business, AVN, we help accountants develop themselves and their practice to a point where it's meeting their definition of successful and enjoyable. We give them hands on workshop style implementation training, resources and tools which shortcut them toward delivering massive value to their clients as well as transforming their own businesses so that they're running a more successful and enjoying accountancy firm.

Through those accountants we're touching hundreds of thousands of business owner's lives who are being better supported and helped in their businesses by the accountants we've helped.

For me, that's making a huge difference, the people behind those businesses are in a position to make better lifestyle choices, whether it's spending more time with family, their hobbies and interests, their health.

Most people don't take the time to define what success means to them and so when I share with them what success means to me, it gives them an understanding of the sort of outcomes I'd like to help them achieve.

Step 3. How your product or service can get them from pain to gain

Few people ever commit any time to look at their business from a bird's-eye view. Your sessions will help them focus on what really matters and come up with improvements.

Describe briefly the areas you'll focus on:

- What's their big dream?

- Getting – and getting more from – customers.

- Improving productivity.

- Getting their life back.

- When would "now" be a good time?

Explain that each session will lead to actionable ideas that take them closer to the business and lifestyle they want.

Step 4. Describe the hierarchical packages you offer

As each client will have an idea of what they're prepared to pay for and how intensive a journey they want to go on, a fixed service may not offer enough for some, but will be too much for others.

Come up with three titles – whether it's gold, silver and bronze or something else entirely – for each level of service and provide a description for each in terms of the time involved and possible outcomes.

Gold, for example, could be a 12-month programme that includes a three-hour session with you every month. The main benefit of this level is the momentum it offers – regular sessions over a year mean that you're with them every step of the way whilst they're implementing actions which will make their business stronger. The outcome is that they'll come away with a minimum of 24 actions. (And remember you'll be quantifying the benefits of each of these).

Next concentrate on the lowest option. Is this a single session? Two sessions? (This level can act as a taster session – at the conclusion of which you can hopefully upsell to the next level – but don't word it as such, otherwise people will choose it over one of your other levels). Explain that the outcomes will be less and you won't necessarily be able to provide them with implementation support, but that they will come away with some clear actions that will have a significant impact on their business.

Finally, describe your silver – or middle – option.

In terms of outcomes for all three, never guarantee results. All you can promise is that they'll come away with increased clarity and some actionable ideas that when implemented will lead to a stronger business.

Step 5. Break the elements down and allocate them to packages

List the features in detail – I've included an example overleaf.

What you get	Bronze One-off session	Silver 6 sessions	Gold 12-month programme
In-depth situation analysis	Yes	Yes	Yes
Plain English Recommendations report after each session	Yes	Yes	Yes
Big picture ideas exploration – leveraging your time	Quick wins	In-depth	In-depth
Getting – and getting more from – customers	Quick wins	In-depth	In-depth
Improving productivity	Quick wins	In-depth	In-depth
How to get your life back	Quick wins	In-depth	In-depth
Powerful monthly one-page report showing exactly how you're doing against your financial and non-financial targets and how you can get better each month	No	No	Yes
Monthly management accounts showing the financial consequences of all your actions	No	No	Yes
Regular hands-on help with implementation and systemisation in your office	No	No	Yes
Working with your team, helping them build systems that will improve efficiency and productivity	No	No	Yes
Powerful monthly sessions to maintain momentum and take your business further	No	No	Yes
Detailed reports covering everything we discuss	Yes	Yes	Yes
"Nagging" – if you want we will nag you to make sure that all your good ideas are turned into actions	Yes	Yes	Yes
100% money back guarantee	Yes	Yes	Yes

Step 6. What it all means

Step five allowed clients to see at a glance what you include in each service level, but now you need to expand on each of the features, explaining what they mean and why they're important. Again, I've given a couple of examples below to help you get started.

In-depth situation analysis

Many business owners don't fully understand where their own business is right now, what it's strengths are and it's weakness nor do they fully appreciate the opportunities the business could seize or the threats it faces as the environment continually changes around them. A carefully structured series of questions helps us form a clear picture of where you are now, so that we can tailor our approach to help you achieve the best results.

Recommendations report written in plain English

After every session we'll agree which of the ideas that we've identified will have the best impact on your business in the shortest amount of time. We'll then type these up into a report and suggest complementary next-step actions.

Step 7. Bolt-ons and their benefits

Here you might want to list any additional services you might offer separately. Perhaps upgrading their typical compliance service to include management accounts that will complement some of the discussions you have.

Perhaps you may want to list some of the items that are bundled into the premium service level separately with a price tag showing that to purchase it independently would be more expensive, thus encouraging people to go for the premium option or at the very least, better positioning the value of it.

Step 8. Case studies and testimonials

Appendix 2 walks you through the process of capturing great case studies and testimonials. Use that process and include them in your brochure.

Step 9. Your closing thoughts
Why you/your business strives for a better world or wants to make a difference.

Make sure you start this with "I believe that..."

> e.g. I believe that a business is a means to an end. It should enable a business owner to live the life he or she deserves to outside of that business. Too many people work incredibly hard to build a business only to regret not being there for their children whilst they were growing up or that their relationship with their spouse has fallen apart in the process. I love helping business owners make a few changes to the way their business is run, which in turn helps them take control of their life again.

By the end of this exercise, you should not only have designed your product, established the support and benefits it includes, and given some thought to your own "why," but also have gained some clarity and confidence on exactly what you can offer clients.

Appendix 2 – How to capture great case studies

Once your client has committed to following the programme, ask if you can capture a brief video of them at each of its stages.

To capture their story on video, you don't need fancy equipment or a camera crew. Simply purchase a small stand for your smartphone – or even rest it against some books – and, if you make a mistake, just carry on. Mistakes, fumbles, ums and ers are all fine – but encourage your client not to swear!

Similarly to finding out the numbers that matter to them, doing this will mean their current situation is uppermost in their minds. If they don't volunteer how they're feeling, ask them. Then ask them to share their thoughts about the session and the impact they believe it might have on their business.

Whenever they've taken action and seen results, capture this too, preferably while their emotion is still fresh.

At the end of the programme go through the numbers with them again to ascertain what's changed – for them and their business – and how they feel about this. Of course, little may have changed, especially if the programme was over a short period or was a single session. Nevertheless, ask them how they believe their business will change now and remember, now is a great time to ask if they wish to continue with more sessions.

Once you've done this it's time to collate all the footage into a case study. Although you could simply put it together in chronological order, you might risk losing your audience's attention. Instead, ascertain your headline result – whether it's that your client's working less hours, or that their sales have soared – then find out what that change means to them and use this as your hook. If, for example, your client has saved an hour per day, how do they spend this? With their children? Their partner? On a new hobby or sport?

Here is my seven-step process for capturing great case studies.

Step 1. Headline
To grab the viewers' attention and encourage them to click 'play,' start by asking clients to share the single biggest change they've experienced as a result of the programme. What has this meant to them? Use this as your headline and the title for your video.

Step 2. Introduction
Ask your client to briefly introduce themselves and their business.

Step 3. Pain
What was their business like before they followed your programme? (You can give them a copy of the 'numbers that matter' sheet to remind them). How did this affect their personal lives and make them feel? What would have been the consequences if things had continued in that way?

Step 4. Journey
What happened to make things better? What specific changes did they make?

Step 5. Outcome
What were the results of these changes? (Ask them to use specific numbers rather than simply stating that things are better). How has this affected their personal life? (Again, focus on the tangible numbers, their emotions and on what they're now able to do).

Step 6. Key insights and tips
Ask what key points they've learned and what they'd recommend to other businesses out there. (Hopefully, this will include a recommendation that they work with you!)

Step 7. Call to action
Now it's your turn. Look straight at the camera and give viewers one clear action to take. Make it a direct command such as "Click the button below this video to discover how I can improve your business and personal life too."

That button might take them to a 'contact us' form. Or perhaps

---

instead you'd rather simply encourage them to phone you.

Now that you've captured a great case study, repurpose it.

As well as putting the finished video on your website and on social media channels such as YouTube and Facebook, you could also:

- Put a TV in your reception area to showcase your growing collection of case studies, or use them during events.

- Extract the audio and use it as your phone system's on-hold recording.

- Have the audio transcribed, send it to your client and ask them to send it back to you on letter headed paper to place in your reception area.

- Create a blog or an article that links back to the video.

- Use specific videos as evidence to show clients who are facing similar challenges that you can help them.

- Once you've built up a repertoire of case studies, use them to write a book!

Appendix 3 – Effective delegation

This resource is taken from System Builder and is designed for an accountant to follow themselves for their practice. Please do use this for yourself but also as a guide when advising your clients on how to delegate.

As a business owner or a manager of a business it's important to be the conductor in the orchestra rather than playing an instrument and certainly rather than trying to do both. Imagine the conductor of an orchestra whose job it is to coordinate all of the musicians to stay on beat, come in when they need to, get louder or softer and whilst doing this simultaneously trying to play the trombone! It would be a disaster! Even though the musicians can read the music and should be able to get on with it. The conductor is a necessary part of the orchestra for coordinating everything and should focus on just that in order to achieve the best possible outcome. So should the business owner or manager of a business. Trying to be all things to all people doesn't work.

Implementing that learning is a little different though. Delegating isn't as easy as just asking someone to do a job for you. It sounds like it should be but more often than not either what we get back isn't what we expected or it doesn't get done at all because we haven't communicated priorities or the importance of the job. This is basically abdication rather than delegation.

Of course, to delegate we don't have to have employees and if you do have employees, you don't have to be restricted to only those employees either. If their workload is maxed out then it doesn't have to come back to you to do the work. You have direct access to millions of people with different skills and experience.

So many people say to me, by the time I've explained how to do this job, I might as well have done it myself. That may well be true. If it's a complete one off and something that can be done quickly then perhaps it is better to do it yourself. How many complete one off jobs to you get and keep getting in? If it's a lot then perhaps recruiting someone with the necessary skills and experience is important.

If it's a job that does come up often then it's worth taking the time now to free up time in the future. Or if it's a one off larger project then it should certainly be delegated.

Firstly, identify the jobs that you can delegate.

1. Refer to **https://www.systembuilder.net/Document/View/797** the action resource 'First things first' which covers quadrants to single out the stuff that you really shouldn't be doing at all and start with those things. (I've shared these with you in the priorisation section).

2. Go through your to do list with someone else, a friend, a colleague and get them to challenge you on why someone else can't do the jobs listed. For many it's difficult to accept that others can do these things or it can be difficult to let go of them. It's easy to convince ourselves that we might as well just get on with them.

Obviously, if you just want someone to nip to the sandwich shop for you then the following isn't so crucial, nor is it for requesting a photocopy of a document 26 times but for the more meaty jobs on your list then this is a great way to effectively delegate them.

Plan the delegation. This process will help you tease the information out of our head to delegate it effectively. It's easy to omit important information that's in your head when delegating which leads to further questions later down the line or the job being done wrong.

There are a number of things that should be considered before the actual delegation takes place.

1. How much does the individual know and need to know about the project to be delegated and it's background? If it's early enough, can they be involved in its planning?

2. Do you care how they do the job? Or just that the job gets done?

e.g. If you've had an idea for an App to be created, do you care what language it's written in or just that it does the job? If how it's done isn't so important then don't be a control freak by telling someone step by step how they should do it unless they need and ask for that level of guidance. Let them use their judgment, experience, skill and brain!

3. If the how it's done is important, create a step-by-step system that they can follow to ensure they don't miss anything. If one doesn't exist and this is going to be a regular occurrence ask them to systemise the process as they work on it. See **https://www.systembuilder.net/Document/View/9963**

4. How much support will you give them along the way? Are you able to? if not, where can they go for support?

5. What's the outcome? Describe what the project you're delegating will look like when it's done. How do you see it, how will others describe it? How will it make your customers feel for example?

6. Why is it important? What's the bigger picture? It may be obvious to you but sometimes when we delegate a piece of work its importance in the grander scheme of things isn't appreciated and so heart and soul aren't put in to it. If it's not important enough to explain, why is it being done in the first place? (I've personally binned off many actions just by going through this process).

7. What are the standards? Depending on the nature of the project there may be standards that need to be considered e.g. Aesthetics, Customer feedback etc.

8. When does it need to be done by, is that realistic and achievable? What happens if it isn't done by then? What are the consequences to the business?

9. Consider at least a couple of milestones where an update is given on its progress. The first one should be very soon so that you can gauge understanding of the project. It's better to check in

early than find that the wrong thing has been worked on for a considerable amount of time.

10. Write all of this down.

Finally, delegate the project/task.

1. Find a distraction free place to speak to the person you're going to delegate the job to.

2. Explain that you have an important job you'd like them to do for you. Talk through the job, why it's important and why you're asking them to do it. (Is it because they're attentive to detail? Incredibly self-driven? Great at motivating people? They're creative? Methodical? What is it about them that gives you comfort in them completing the project?)

3. Explain what the project is and if it's applicable to explain the process and whether you want them to create systems around it.

4. Discuss the deadline and the milestones (and what you expect to see at each milestone), ask if they're comfortable with the dates.

5. Understand what their other priorities are and then agree with them where your project fits within those other priorities. Is it at the top or should they drop yours to deal with something else if it comes up.

6. Ask them to talk you through in their own words what the project is, why it's important and what the outcomes are. Ensure this isn't fed back parrot fashion but that it's clear they understand. Ask questions.

7. Put the milestone and deadline dates in your computer diaries so that it pops up on both screens at the right time. Make sure you attend the update meeting otherwise the project will be undervalued.

8. Give them a copy of the document you've filled in. Do this at

---

the end so that they're not simply reading from it instead of listening to you and also that they don't read the content back when you seek to ensure understanding.

Action to take:

Use the template on the opposite page. It will help you define the delegation process. Pick 1 medium sized project from your list (i.e. not a sandwich shop run!) and go through this process right now.

Delegation Guide

Skills/knowledge/experience required:	
Delegated to:	Delegated from:
Why is this important? And what are the consequences to the business of this not happening?	
Why I'm entrusting it to you:	
My vision of what this looks like complete:	
The standards that have to be met:	
Rules/Guiding Principles:	
A System exists?	A System is needed?
Here's how I'd like it done:	
The best person(s) to see for support:	
I'd like to see the initial progress on this project on (date and time):	I need this completed no later than:
Other milestones and expected progress:	

Appendix 4 – Free help from AVN

I'm genuinely worried for the accountancy profession as a whole. Many don't perceive the threat that looms but will do and sooner than you might think. AVN's mission is to help UK accountancy practices become the most successful and enjoyable to run.

In an effort to help more and more accountants, AVN have created a free step by step programme that gives you world class training, tools and guidance to help you improve your profits, cashflow, average fees, service levels and client base. Use as much or as little as you want, it's completely free. Just visit **www.improveyourpractice.co.uk** to get instant access.

Appendix 5 – About the author

Since the early 90's Shane Lukas has worked with a variety of businesses putting systems and processes in place that improve the overall efficiency and productivity of those businesses.

Since 1998 Shane has been part of AVN and since 2007 the Managing Director of the business, helping accountants build a stronger, more successful and profitable practice and helping them deliver much greater value to the business owners they work with; helping their business owner clients run much more profitable, successful and enjoyable businesses and importantly, regain control of their lives too – giving accountants a much greater sense of purpose.

Shane Lukas is author of the book – 'The Business Owner's Guide to the UK's Best Accountancy Practices' – a book that describes how AVN Accountants can deliver significantly more value than traditional accountants. And co-author of the book 'The World's Most Inspiring Accountants' – a book which demonstrates the life changing impact accountants can have on their clients by simply spending more valuable time with them.

Please do connect with Shane in any of the following ways...

Linked in: **www.Linkedin.com/in/SLUKAS**

Tap in to additional learning and get access to world class training and resources via **www.improveyourpractice.co.uk**

Send an email and chat with Shane via **shane.lukas@avn.co.uk**